BEYOND
GENUINE STUPIDITY
Ensuring AI Serves Humanity

BEYOND GENUINE STUPIDITY

First published in United Kingdom and United States of America by

Fast Future Publishing in 2017

http://www.fastfuture.com

For Information contact info@fastfuture.com

Paperback ISBN 978-0-9932958-7-4

eBook ISBN 978-0-9932958-6-7

Cover Designed by Dusan Arsenic

Interior design and typesetting by April Koury

Print production by Print Trail

BEYOND GENUINE STUPIDITY

Ensuring AI Serves Humanity

Authors

Rohit Talwar
Steve Wells
Alexandra Whittington
April Koury
Maria Romero

Edited by

Rohit Talwar and Maria Romero

www.fastfuture.com

ABOUT FAST FUTURE

Fast Future is a professional foresight firm specializing in delivering keynote speeches, executive education, research, and consulting on the emerging future and the impacts of change for global clients. We publish books from leading future thinkers around the world, exploring how developments such as AI, robotics, exponential technologies, and disruptive thinking could impact individuals, societies, businesses, and governments and create the trillion-dollar sectors of the future. Fast Future has a particular focus on ensuring these advances are harnessed to unleash individual potential and enable a very human future.

www.fastfuture.com
Twitter @fastfuture @futrbiz
www.facebook.com/FutrBiz/
www.linkedin.com/company/fast-future-publishing/

THE AUTHORS

Rohit Talwar is a global futurist, award-winning keynote speaker, author, and the CEO of Fast Future. His prime focus is on helping clients understand and shape the emerging future by putting people at the center of the agenda. Rohit is the co-author of *Designing Your Future*, lead editor and a contributing author for *The Future of Business*, editor of *Technology vs. Humanity*, and co-editor and contributor for the forthcoming books: *Unleashing Human Potential – The Future of AI in Business*, and *50:50 – Scenarios for the Next 50 Years*.

rohit@fastfuture.com
Twitter @fastfuture
www.facebook.com/RohitKTalwar
www.linkedin.com/in/talwar

Steve Wells is an experienced strategist, keynote speaker, futures analyst, partnership working practitioner, and the COO of Fast Future. He has a particular interest in helping clients anticipate and respond to the disruptive bursts of technological possibility that are shaping the emerging future. Steve is a co-editor of *The Future of Business*, *Technology vs. Humanity*, and forthcoming books on *Unleashing Human Potential – The Future of AI in Business* and *50:50 – Scenarios for the Next 50 Years*.

steve@fastfuture.com
Twitter @informingchoice
www.facebook.com/stevewells.futurist
www.linkedin.com/in/wellssteve/

Alexandra Whittington is a futurist, writer, foresight director of Fast Future, and faculty member on the Futures program at the University of Houston. She has a particular expertise in future visioning and scenario planning. Alexandra is a contributor to *The Future of Business* and a co-editor for forthcoming books on *Unleashing Human Potential – The Future of AI in Business* and *50:50 – Scenarios for the Next 50 Years*.

alex@fastfuture.com
Twitter @alexandra4casts
www.linkedin.com/in/alexandra-whittington-86794876

April Koury is a foresight researcher, writer, and the publishing director of Fast Future. She has worked on a range of foresight initiatives including society and media in 2020, emerging economies, and the future of travel, tourism, and transportation. April is a co-editor of *The Future of Business, Technology vs. Humanity,* and two forthcoming books on *Unleashing Human Potential – The Future of AI in Business* and *50:50 – Scenarios for the Next 50 Years*.

april@fastfuture.com
www.linkedin.com/in/april-koury-20b04396/

Maria Romero was a futurist and foresight researcher at Fast Future. She has worked on a range of foresight initiatives including a project for NASA's Langley Research Center and the publication of "The Future of Student Life: Living" in *On The Horizon*. Maria is a contributor to *Unleashing Human Potential – The Future of AI in Business*.

info@fastfuture.com
www.linkedin.com/in/mgromerom/

Contents

Introduction

By Rohit Talwar and Maria Romero

Beyond Genuine Stupidity – Ensuring AI Serves Humanity is aimed at the business leaders of today and tomorrow, those whose lives might be impacted by artificial intelligence (AI) in the years ahead, and interested onlookers. Our aim is to explore critical issues arising from the rapid pace of development of AI and to highlight the need for an enlightened, forward-looking, and holistic approach to ensuring that this most disruptive of technologies is harnessed in service of humanity. We hope you enjoy reading it and welcome your feedback. This is the first book in the *Fast Future* series—which is designed to provide clear and rapid insights into the trends, forces, developments, and ideas shaping the future and the possible scenarios that could arise.

Just Another Disruptive Technology?

Almost every new technology arrives with a fanbase claiming it will revolutionize life on Earth. For some, AI is just one more in a long list of over-hyped technologies that won't live up to its promise. At the other end of the spectrum are those who believe this could literally be the game changing invention that reshapes our world. They argue that humanity has a directional choice: Do we want the transformation to enable an unleashing of human potential, or lead us towards the effective end of life on the planet? We believe AI is like no technology that has gone before, but we are far too early in its evolution to know how far and how rapidly this Fourth Industrial Revolution powered by smart machines might spread.

What is clear is that, in real terms, although we are only in the very early stages of the AI revolution, we can already see that it has the potential to disrupt every aspect of our private and public lives. Indeed, AI is already having a dramatic impact across everything from medical diagnosis and construction to government decision making, financial services, and even dating sites. As the pace of development accelerates, and AI's potential becomes a little clearer, so the warnings grow ever-stronger about the threat to jobs and privacy, and the risks of humanity becoming enslaved by the machine.

Beyond Genuine Stupidity - Ensuring AI Serves Humanity

We argue here that humanity cannot risk sleep walking into a future where human choice and opportunity have been eroded, and individuals, society, businesses, and governments are ill-prepared for the consequences. Arguably the best way to confront this is by becoming smart about both the impacts and governance of AI at every level. Hence, we believe the time is right to overcome short-termist thinking and the sensationalist marketing hype. In short, across society, we need to deepen our understanding of the nature and potential impacts of AI and its disruptive technology companions. Armed with that understanding, we can start preparing for a range of possible futures, and experimenting with solutions for the challenges ahead— this is the motivation behind *Beyond Genuine Stupidity – Ensuring AI Serves Humanity.*

Clearly, in a world where the news cycle has been reduced to hours or minutes, thinking about the long-term has become an unusual and difficult activity. In a fast-changing world with a rapidly changing reality, it is no surprise that as individuals, businesses, and even governments, we are often only planning for the next month, quarter, or year. However, the far-reaching and seemingly limitless potential applications, impacts, and implications of AI demand that we look more deeply into the opportunities and challenges that an AI-enabled future might bring. This book is designed to provide a rapid exploration of the emerging applications and implications of

AI across society and to highlight what an intelligent approach to the issues might look like—in short, how can we ensure that we go *Beyond Genuine Stupidity* in preparing for artificial intelligence.

So, What is Artificial Intelligence?

Essentially, AI is a computer science discipline that seeks to create intelligent software and hardware that can replicate our critical mental faculties in order to work and react like humans. Key applications include speech recognition, language translation, visual perception, learning, reasoning, inference, strategizing, planning, decision making, and intuition. There are several underlying disciplines encompassed within the field of AI, including big data, data mining, rules-based (expert) systems, neural networks, fuzzy logic, machine learning (ML), deep learning (DL), generative adversarial networks, cognitive computing, natural language processing (NLP), robotics, and the recognition of speech, images, and video.

Those developing AI tools and applications draw on a diverse set of underlying disciplines including cognition, computer science, mathematics, statistics, linguistics, philosophy, psychology, and neuroscience. More recently, those in the field have also been looking to the biological, chemical, and material sciences for ideas and approaches that could help deliver ever-smarter systems.

Some AI applications have been with us for over thirty years, such as simple rules-based expert systems for credit scoring in financial services. Machine vision and robotics have also been in use in some form for over two decades in manufacturing. More recently the field of AI has received a major boost due to a combination of factors, namely:

- The need to process the massive data stores being accumulated by all businesses and the major online players such as Google and Facebook in particular;
- Ever-faster computing hardware, including parallel processing architectures;
- The spread of cloud computing and network connectivity;
- Major advances in the design of neural networks and machine

learning algorithms;

- The decentralization of AI, with hundreds of thousands, if not millions, of developers building tools, applications, and new AI start-ups; and,
- The sheer scale of investment in AI by major technology companies and investors.

As a result, we have seen a massive expansion of AI tools, applications, and new businesses, with the majority centered on the use of some form of ML or DL algorithms. Most current applications are delivering so called "Narrow AI"—targeting a specific area of activity such as cancer diagnosis or facial recognition. In contrast, "Deep AI" is generally considered by some as the true purist goal of AI—developing systems that can display artificial general intelligence (AGI)—mirroring human capacity across a range of domains.

There are many in the AI field who believe that AGI is only a stepping stone on the path to artificial superintelligence (ASI), which would deliver smart machines that can far outstrip the capabilities of the human mind. Such AGI and ASI developments could go well beyond the bounds of our current understanding. We could see them creating new political systems, alternative economic management models, fields of science that we cannot even conceive of today, and potentially even new lifeforms.

While AI is without a doubt becoming the brains behind many of the most impactful innovations on the horizon, its full potential only truly emerges when it is combined with a range of other science and technology developments that are also progressing at an exponential rate. These include augmented reality, autonomous vehicles, big data, biomimicry, blockchain, cloud computing, DNA computing, drones, genetics, human brain and body enhancements, hyperconnectivity, the Internet of things, nanotechnology, smart materials, organic and synthetic chemistry, quantum computing, renewable energy, robotics, sensors, synthetic biology, virtual reality, and 3D/4D printing.

A Revolution in the Making?

Behind all these technical definitions and enabling factors lies one the most transformational concepts humanity has ever created. In fact, some experts have started to agree with author James Barrat who described AI technology as "Our final invention." What sets AI aside from all other innovations in history is its ability to learn and evolve autonomously. So, while previous machines and software have followed instructions, AI can make its own decisions, execute a growing range of tasks, and increasingly, update its own knowledge base and code.

Unquantifiable Economic Impact?

As with past economic shifts, successive waves of AI-enabled automation of tasks and processes are expected to drive technological unemployment. Projections and forecasts abound of AI's potential impact in both eliminating and generating jobs. There are also numerous attempts being made to predict the resulting overall level of employment at a national and global level, and where the skill shortages and surpluses might be in the coming decades. In practice, the employment outlook will be shaped by the combination of the Fourth Industrial Revolution, the decisions of powerful corporations and investors, the requirements of current and "yet to be born" future industries and businesses, an unpredictable number of economic cycles, and the policies of national governments and supra-national institutions.

Collectively, the diverse economic factors at play here mean it is simply too complex a challenge to predict with any certainty what the likely progress of job creation and displacement might be across the planet over the next two decades. Across the world, many of the analysts, forecasters, economists, developers, scientists, and technology providers involved in the jobs debate are also largely missing or avoiding a key point here. In their contributions, they either don't understand, or are deliberately failing to emphasize, the self-evolving and accelerated learning capability of AI and its potentially dramatic impact on society. If we do get to true AGI or ASI, then it is hard to see what jobs might left for the humans. Hence, through the pages of this book, we argue that perhaps a more intelligent approach is to start preparing for a range of possible scenarios.

Human Futures Reimagined?

For individuals, the current political and economic uncertainties may have served to create a sense that this is way beyond our understanding or control, and so we narrow our vision of the future. Alarmist reports in the media around AI can lead people to feel desperately hopeless. At the same time, we hear some political leaders justifying governmental inaction. They argue that, as with past technological disruptions, things will resolve themselves through the market, and that everyone will benefit from the resulting improvements in productivity and growth. Finally, many vendors, while hyping their products on the one hand, are also largely sidestepping the employment and social impact issues by suggesting that AI will augment rather than replace humans.

The net result of the mixed messages from the media, government, and businesses is that individuals are often either overwhelmed or lulled into a false sense of security, instead of feeling inspired and encouraged to act to take a pro-active approach to managing their future. The harsh reality is that everyone needs to understand the disruptive nature of AI, and that if it does fulfill its true potential, then this goes well beyond the idea of "the end of jobs as we know them". Indeed, as we explore in this book, this is just the tip of the iceberg, and AI has the potential to redefine every human activity from life-partner selection, smart cities, and autonomous self-owning vehicles to robotic farming, fully automated legal systems, and AI-designed lifeforms. Hence, we argue that people around the world should take control of their destinies by learning new skills, which would help them secure a better future for them and their loved ones. The transition might be painful, but if we ensure AI serves humanity, the future could be one of abundance for everyone.

Emergence of New Societal Structures?

Right now, many in society are blissfully unaware of how AI could alter key social structures. For example, if the legal system could be administered and enforced by AI, would this mean that we have reached the ideals of fair access, objectivity, and impartiality? Or, on the contrary, would the inherent and unintended bias of its creators define the new order? If no one has to work for a living, would children still need to go to school? How would people spend their new found permanent free time? Without traditional notions of employment, how will people pay for housing, goods, and services?

For wider society, what might the impacts of large-scale redundancies across all professions mean for the prevalence of mental health issues? Would societies become more human or more technical as a result of the pervasiveness of AI? How would we deal with privacy and security concerns? What are the implications for notions such as family, community, and the rule of law? These are just a few of the key topics where the application of AI could have direct and unintended consequences that challenge our current assumptions and working models and will therefore need to be addressed in the not so distant future. An inclusive, experimental, and proactive response to these challenges would help ensure that we are not blindsided by the impacts of change and that no segment of society gets left behind.

New Challenges for Business and Government?

With many technologies in recent history, businesses have had the luxury of knowing that they can wait until they were ready to pursue their adoption. For most firms, they could be relatively safe in the assumption that being late to market wouldn't necessarily mean their demise. Furthermore, a predominantly short-term, results driven focus and culture has led to many ignoring or trivializing AI because it is "too soon to know," or worse "it will never happen." Finally, those at the top of larger firms are rarely that excited by any technology, and can struggle to appreciate the truly disruptive potential of AI.

However, the exponential speed of AI developments means that the pause for thought may have to be a lot shorter. There's a core issue of digital literacy here, and the more data-centric our businesses become, the greater the imperative to start by investing time to understand and analyze the technology. From the top down, we need to appreciate how AI compares to and differs from previous disruptive advancements, and grasp its capability to enable new and previously unimaginable ideas and business models. Within our businesses, we need to understand the potential for AI to unlock value from the vast arrays of data we are amassing by the second. We also need to become far more conscious of the longer-term societal impact and the broader role of business in society.

Call it corporate social responsibility or enlightened self-interest, but either way, businesses will have to think much more strategically about the broader societal ramifications of operational decisions. Where will the money come from for people to buy our goods and services if, like us, firms in every sector are reducing their headcounts in favor of automation? What is our responsibility to the people we lay off? How should we respond to the notion of robot taxes? How could we assure the right balance between humans and machines so the technology serves people?

Clearly there is some desire in business today to augment human capability and free up the time of our best talent through the application of AI. However, the evidence suggests that the vast majority of AI projects are backed by a business case predicated on reducing operational costs—largely in the form of humans. Some are already raising concerns that such a narrowly focused pursuit of cost efficiency through automation may limit our capacity to respond to problems and changing customer needs. Humans are still our best option when it comes to adapting to new developments, learning about emerging industries, pursuing new opportunities, and innovating to stay abreast or ahead of the competition in a fast-changing world. Business leaders must weigh up the benefits of near-term cost-savings and taking humanity out of the business, against the risk of automating to the point of commoditizing our offerings.

Governments are clearly seeing the potential—and some of the risks and consequences of AI. For example, in its November 22nd, 2017 budget statement, the UK government announced plans to invest around US$660 million in AI, broadband, and 5G technology and a further US$530 million to support the introduction of electric autonomous vehicles. However, they are also confronted by tough choices on how to deal with the myriad issues that already starting to arise: Who should own the technology and its likely power? What measures will be needed to deal with the potential rise of unemployment? Should we be running pilot projects for guaranteed basic incomes and services? Should we be considering robot taxes? What changes will be required to the academic curriculum? What support is required by adult learners to retrain for new roles? How can we increase the accessibility and provision of training, knowledge, and economic support for new ventures?

A side effect that is often overlooked in the discussion of AI is the potential for increased levels of stress, depression, and broader mental health issues. With these issues already on the rise in many nations, some see them as an inevitable outcome of the ever increasing uncertainty and frustration of potentially losing your job and not having enough money to provide for your dependents, or to simply live your life the way you want. The challenge here is for forward-thinking governments to seize the baton and start preparing for a range of possible consequences of the technologies they are investing in.

Chapter Introductions

Beyond Genuine Stupidity – Ensuring AI Serves Humanity is a compilation of the Fast Future team's latest thinking on AI and its impacts across society. The book presents a total of twenty-six chapters divided into four sections—each covering specific points of impact: society, industries, businesses, and jobs and economy. For your convenience, we have summarized the content of each chapter below.

Impacts of AI on Society

1. *Artificial Intelligence – Five Societal Priorities*: Recommendations on critical actions to absorb and adapt to the changes brought about by exponential technological advances.

2. *Technological Disruption – A Survival Guide*: Highlights strategies that governments should experiment with right now to prepare society for the possibility of large-scale technological

unemployment.

3. *Living with the Enemy – Staying Human in the Era of Super-intelligent Machines*: A reflection on how to navigate the evolving relationship between humans and smart machines in the coming decades, encompassing workplace changes, job opportunities, products and services, business models, and management.

4. *Morning, Noon and Night – 15 Ways AI Could Transform Daily Life*: Discusses day-to-day activities, behaviors, and habits that could be altered by AI, from wardrobe management to community building.

5. *How Artificial Intelligence Might Help Us Decode Our World*: An exploration of the possible personal impacts of AI when applied to dating, family, friendships, and career planning in the future.

6. *The Human, Smart, and Sustainable Future of Cities*: Presents a big picture perspective on the journey cities must navigate to become vision-led, citizen-centered, smart, integrated, green, and sustainable.

Impacts of AI on Major Industries

7. *AI and Health Care – The Now, The Next, and The Possible*: A scenario timeline for the future of AI-enabled healthcare systems.

8. *The Creative and Destructive Impacts of AI-Powered FinTech on Financial Services*: Exploring the possible consequences of applying AI as a service combined with other FinTech applications in financial services.

9. *Riding Shotgun with Autonomous Vehicles*: Exploring the opportunities and implications of self-driving cars in relation to insurance, accident rates, fuel management, traffic flows, and taxi services.

10. *Robo-Retail vs. Humanity at a Price? – Two Possible Futures for Retail*: Sets out contrasting alternative scenarios for the level

and pace of retail sector automation.

11. *Unleashing the True Potential of AI – Building the Exponential Law Firm*: A comprehensive summary of the potential of AI to unlock transformative growth across the legal sector.

12. *A Day in the Life of a Legal Project Manager: June 1st, 2020*: A chronicle of the future that portrays the deep integration of AI into the legal workplace.

13. *Most Exponential Law Firms 2025*: A leap into a selection of plausible exponential growth strategies in tomorrow's legal sector.

14. *Artificial Intelligence and the Growth Opportunity for Accounting Firms*: A snapshot of how the accounting sector can benefit from disruptions in the economic system and in business resulting from the adoption of AI and other exponential technologies.

15. *Designing for a Post-Job Future: The Impact of AI on Architecture*: Highlighting examples of how the deployment of AI could help transform design thinking for the built environment.

16. *AI and the Many Possible Futures of the IT Professional*: An image of the future that travels from 2019 to 2025 showing the possible evolution of an IT professional's role in an increasingly AI-enabled world.

17. *Artificial Intelligence – The Next Frontier in IT Security?*: A short overview of the ways AI could support humans in protecting ever-more complex systems.

Impacts of AI on Business

18. *Artificial Intelligence in the Workplace – The Leadership Challenge*: Examines critical implications of the Fourth Industrial Revolution for business management, outlining five key leadership priorities.

19. *AI – Addressing the Human and Workplace Implications*: How we can ensure a human-centered perspective in the future design of work and workplaces.

20. *Hope is Not a Strategy – Retention, Engagement, and Productivity in the Era of Artificial Intelligence*: A discussion of how we might manage, motivate, reward, and retain our best performers.

21. *Small Business and AI: Now, Next, and Future*: Exploration over three time horizons of how small to medium enterprises might embrace the potential of AI.

Impacts of AI on Jobs and the Economy

22. *Dancing with Disruption – 20 Jobs that Could Be Transformed by AI*: Twenty examples of how AI could transform job roles across society by 2030.

23. *Hand Picked by Robots – The Beginning of the End for Humans in the Food Sector?*: A short study of how jobs in the food and beverage industry might evolve with the development of AI.

24. *Rethinking Work and Jobs in the Exponential Era*: A review of future unemployment projections and forecasts, and an exploration of the resulting skills and management challenges.

25. *Hire the Robots, Free the People*: Outlines a plausible scenario of a future without jobs where humans are unleashed to fulfill their unlimited potential.

26. *Taxing the Robots – Far Sighted or Fanciful?*: An overview of the key drivers, questions, challenges, and implementation issues associated with introducing robot taxes to cover the costs of AI-induced technological unemployment.

IMPACTS OF AI
ON SOCIETY

Artificial Intelligence – Five Societal Priorities

By Rohit Talwar, Steve Wells, and Alexandra Whittington

How can we ensure that advances in science and technology are harnessed to secure the betterment of all humanity?

If aliens visited Earth, we'd expect to witness world changing technologies with capabilities beyond our imaginations—blurring the boundaries between reality, fiction, and magic. Even without the aliens, artificial intelligence (AI) is displaying the ability and potential for dramatic disruption—promising deep-rooted impacts across sectors, from manufacturing and transport (think driverless vehicles) to education and mental health.

The future applications of AI are limitless and unknowable—we are too early in its evolution to know how far it could replicate and ultimately exceed the human brain's capabilities. Predicting the reactions of humans, businesses, governments, and civil society is almost impossible as there is limited understanding of AI's potential or willingness to think deeply about impacts and consequences. Forecasts vary of how many jobs could be replaced or created through the adoption of AI and its sister technologies.

Whether 80% of jobs are eliminated or 50% more created, the new jobs will require advanced skillsets and mindsets. The transition will be dramatic, painful, and require new knowledge and competences. Governments, businesses, and civil society will need to rethink the assumptions and mechanisms that underpin our world. We believe five areas should be central to societal discourse, business strategy, and government policy in order to avoid inevitable shocks and crises: raising technological literacy, ownership of technological innovation, micro-business creation, ensuring technological advances serve humanity, and the consequences to health and well-being.

An ill-prepared society is possibly the biggest risk. To prepare for change we must understand its drivers. Government ministers, business leaders, front line staff, teachers, and parents need to understand the science and technology developments shaping the future and the new ways of thinking, business models, and game-changing ideas they enable. This is a personal responsibility and something firms and governments could address through in-service training and adult education offerings. Free and cheap online platforms already provide the content—the challenge is encouraging access and building it into both personal development and back to work programs.

A deeper understanding of AI in particular would clarify why so many experts and commentators are raising concerns about ownership of critical future technologies. There are warnings that a few highly powerful investors and corporations could literally dominate and dictate life on Earth. The fear is that they will develop and own the core technologies and applications that underpin every business activity, government decision, social interaction, and financial exchange. Some argue for strict controls on the extent of such intellectual property (IP) monopolies. Others suggest the IP for critical technologies such as AI should be taken into public ownership and made available for firms of all sizes to access, possibly paying a revenue share into public funds to finance future developments and the costs of basic income and service provision to those displaced by automation.

Today, we have no idea of how many jobs automation will displace over the next decade. We can though make reasonable assumptions that large numbers of tasks will be automated—even in professions such as medicine, law, and finance. It is also hard to estimate the scale of total task replacement. For example, would safer autonomous vehicles mean the beginning of the end for repair garages and auto insurance policies as the manufacturers or even the cars themselves seek to cover their own reduced liabilities?

The one certainty is that people will need to take more responsibility for their incomes through the creation of small and micro-businesses. Employers can play a massive role here in providing start-up training and mentoring through the early phases of business creation for employees they are replacing with technology. The most forward thinking might even co-invest with such businesses to help them get started and potentially provide them with a route to market. Governments could provide similar services and easy-to-use online platforms for business creation, marketing, networking, financial management, invoicing, accounting, and tax submission, enabling founders to focus on the development of their business.

Finally, the threat or reality of technological replacement is already adversely impacting physical health and mental well-being across a range of occupations. An accelerating pace of change seems likely to exacerbate this. Online tools could help people deal with stress in a confidential manner and help train the next generation of mental health professionals.

Clearly, the accelerating pace of technological development could bring significant benefits. There are also genuine concerns about the potential for dehumanization of those left behind as wealth and power becomes consolidated into the hands of the few. There will inevitably be concerns over raising taxation to fund all this—to which the counter-question would be how will we fund the consequences of failing to prepare and inaction?

- *What key impacts of AI should society be preparing for today?*
- *How can we prepare adults and children for a world where technology will perform roles traditionally undertaken by humans?*
- *What role should the state play in governing the deployment of disruptive technologies?*

A version of this article was originally published in *The Financial Times* under the title "Securing a Very Human Future."

Technological Disruption –
A Survival Guide

By Rohit Talwar, Steve Wells, and Alexandra Whittington

How can individuals, governments, and businesses prepare for the inevitable technological disruptions of the next twenty years?

Technology and the ways we use it promise to disrupt society and business in dramatic ways. Should we wait for future shocks before we respond—or are there practical steps we can take to prepare us for a range of possible outcomes and increase our resilience in the face of uncertainty? This article explores practical steps we can take now to prepare for the inevitable surprises.

Fundamental changes are taking place in the way organizations are using technology. Many are embarking on radical digital overhauls to enable them to deliver new offerings, enhance service, improve efficiency, and increase cost competitiveness. The process of digital transformation is likely to spread across the business world, and the harsh reality is that wide-scale automation will inevitably lead to job reductions across everything from mining and retail to education and the accounting sector.

In parallel, new sectors are of course emerging and creating opportunities—but no one yet knows if they will generate enough jobs to replace those displaced by technology. Some estimates suggest that over the next 20 years up to 80% of all current jobs could be digitized; others estimate that for every new job created, three to four could be eliminated elsewhere. The truth is that it's impossible to know how the situation will play out in the next two to three years let alone with the waves of change shaping the next 20. A good example of this is the uncertainty over Brexit for the United Kingdom (UK) and European Union (EU). The situation is changing literally by the day and so it becomes almost impossible to think about what the longer term outcome might be.

The future could be a very exciting place where we tackle a lot of current challenges in society and create new opportunities. New industry sectors such as laboratory grown food, vertical farming, autonomous vehicles, clean water technologies, renewable energy, and synthetic materials all hold out great possibilities for humanity. However, these businesses will be highly automated from the outset, and will require very different capabilities and a highly skilled workforce. The transition to these new roles will not be smooth for the production worker, shift manager, warehouse assistant, sales person, truck driver, or even lawyer whose jobs are at risk.

While there might be a temptation and tendency to "wait and see" because the challenges seem so immense—this could be calamitously risky. The change, when it happens, will cascade and accelerate rapidly, leaving unprepared governments, businesses, societies, and individuals overwhelmed and paralyzed. We believe it is far better to anticipate impending shocks and risks and act now to start putting society on a more sustainable footing, thus ensuring it is resilient enough to cope with the risk of large-scale technological unemployment.

We believe there are five fundamental actions that forward-looking governments should be taking right now.

1. Experimenting with Guaranteed Basic Incomes and Services

The firms undertaking job automation need customers to buy their goods and services. Hence, we see many in Silicon Valley arguing for some form of automation tax to fund the provision of universal guaranteed basic incomes (UBI) and services (UBS) to everyone in society. Some governments refuse to countenance the idea on ideological grounds because they think it reeks of communism. However, others are recognizing that something needs to be done to avoid large-scale social decline and potential citizen unrest. Hence, many countries including Finland, Germany, and Canada are undertaking UBI experiments to understand the concept, assess the social impact, measure the costs, and prepare themselves while they still have time.

2. A Massive Expansion of Support for Start-Up Creation

People will inevitably have to take more control of their own destiny. One way is to create their own job or small business that is far more immune to risks of technology replacing humans. A massive expansion of support for start-up creation would both generate jobs for the mentors and accelerate the rate at which people can build new businesses and create new jobs.

3. Research and Development in Key Knowledge Sectors

A competitive economy demands cutting edge innovation. A safe society requires research and development on the materials and processes that will enable that innovation to happen without adverse social consequences. Not all R&D lends itself to assessment based on the return on investment—some just has to be undertaken for the betterment of society. Hence, expanding research funding and the number of research institutions and posts are important enablers of tomorrow's job creation.

4. Rethinking Education at Every Level

Success in the future will require a smart, adaptable, and highly educated workforce. Indeed, many commentators and some governments anticipate that within a decade, most new jobs will require a graduate level of education as a minimum. How that is acquired may well look very different to today.

To survive and thrive we think and believe everyone will need to understand both the technologies and the mindsets shaping the future. There are lots of technological competitors to Uber and Airbnb: For the latter, their true point of difference is their mindset, a radically different way of thinking about how you deliver on customer desires without owning any assets or employing any of the service delivery staff. We also need to help people develop higher-level skills that will help them learn rapidly and transition into and between jobs that don't even exist today. These skills include collaboration, problem solving, navigating complexity, scenario thinking, and accelerated learning.

Therefore, we believe we need a massive increase in the provision of free adult education using existing facilities at schools and higher education institutions for delivery—most of the teaching spaces are unused in the evening. We also need to reduce pupil-teacher ratios at school level to help with personalized support because the evidence is clear on the impact. This also means looking at the charges imposed on students pursuing higher education: We need a well-educated workforce to propel the country forward. Many other nations are providing free degree level education—globally, we need sustainable solutions that don't leave future generations demotivated, disillusioned, and saddled with debts that they cannot repay.

5. Addressing the Mental Health Challenge

Across society, the scale and severity of mental health issues is rising. Large-scale job displacement will only increase that. An enlightened approach would be to provide far richer workplace support for those suffering mental health challenges, and to fund people to train as therapists while still working today so that they will be ready to help when the challenge becomes a major problem in two to four years' time.

There's clearly a cost associated with enabling all these activities, but we have to ask ourselves what the risks and potential costs of inaction might be. A short term saving on costs could lead to a very long-term increase in the cost of funding unemployment benefits and policing a society that feels let down.

- *What could be the long term societal and economic impacts of near term inaction?*

- *How should we prioritize what needs to be done? Where should we start?*

- *How can we shift the prevailing paradigm from return on investment to betterment of society?*

Living with the Enemy – Staying Human in the Era of Superintelligent Machines

By Rohit Talwar, Steve Wells, and Alexandra Whittington

How can we ensure a very human future in the face of ever bleaker warnings about the impact of technological progress on humanity?

Turn to any media outlet today, and you will see concerns being expressed about super-intelligent technology taking over the planet, and whether this means that humanity is on a one-way path to irrelevance?

In response, it has been fascinating to watch the rhetoric of technology companies evolve in recent times from heralding the potential of technologies such as artificial intelligence (AI) to automate processes and reduce staff costs, to a new story line of "augmented intelligence"—arguing that the machines are here to serve not replace us. Why? The reality is that throughout history, turkeys have steadfastly refused to vote for an early Christmas. So, from business leaders to front line employees, the penny is dropping with an ever-louder and more resonant thud. The realization is growing that—unlike previous industrial revolutions and waves of technological change—this time it's different. Hence, in the face of rising concerns about the impact on jobs and society, the technologists are in damage limitation mode pretending that their technological Ferraris are just pushbikes with the addition of a shopping basket and mud guards.

So, what's really going on? Whilst it is far too early to know or predict the true potential and resulting impact of AI, it is clear that it will have widespread applications and deep ramifications across society. These include scenarios such as the end of jobs as a mainstream income-generating activity, the rise of state guaranteed incomes, the emergence of fully automated decentralized autonomous organizations (DAOs) with no employees, and a massive shift in societal norms and culture if leisure becomes the prime use of our time. To help explore these next waves of change, below we address six key questions on the rise of these disruptive exponential technologies, the impact on humanity, and how we can ensure a very human future in the age of superintelligent machines.

Q1. How might we prepare for changing relationship between humans and machines over the next 10-20 years?

As we look at the changes shaping our world and the pace of technological advancement, some very big questions start to arise:

- Are humans irrelevant to the future of business?
- What role should humans play when machines can outperform them in most tasks?
- How should society prepare for an unknowable future?

We see five important dimensions that we must address as part of securing humanity's future in an automated world and ensuring that the advances in technology are used to serve humanity—not replace it.

Reframing Society – We are reaching a truly dramatic point in human history where a number of exponential technologies are being combined to deliver radical performance improvements. A powerful mix of unleashed imaginations applied to disruptive technologies is catalyzing a possibility revolution across every aspect of human life, society, government, and business. As a result, in the next few years, society will be challenged to confront fundamental issues that go to the core of what it means to be human. Advances in science and technology will test every assumption we have about how our world works and the purpose of humans within it. For example, AI already outperforms humans in many domains, and the possibility of "artificial superintelligence," or constantly learning and evolving systems, could result in machines capable of overtaking human capabilities—ultimately even in so-called soft skills such as empathy, intuition, and creativity.

Humanity 2.0 – We are now able to augment our capabilities using advances such as cognitive enhancement drugs and nootropic supplements, electronic brain stimulation techniques, genetics, age extension treatments, 3D printed limbs and organs, and body worn exoskeletons. These have given rise to the notion of enhancing the human brain and body well beyond the limits of natural evolutionary processes.

Indeed, many leaders in the field of AI are fierce advocates of "Transhumanism" as the next stage of human evolution. They argue that if humans want to keep up with AI, we ourselves will have to become machines, embedding technology in our brains and bodies to give us similar levels of processing power. So, is there a meaningful future for version 1.0 humans in this brave new and enhanced world that the techno-progressives would have us believe is the only viable way forward for humanity? Will we have to enhance ourselves if we want to be considered for one of the potentially declining number of jobs that might be available?

The Risks of Automation – The challenge here lies in our choices as decision makers and the value we place on human attributes that machines cannot as yet replicate. Clearly, automation has many benefits such as cost efficiency, consistency, speed, and accuracy. Many firms will inevitably choose to place their faith in computer systems, automating wherever possible. Such a philosophy is common in new technology ventures where the heart of the business is embedded in its code. Some are already creating entities that have no employees and exist entirely in software.

The potential rewards of widespread digitization of an enterprise are well-covered in the business media, but what isn't talked about enough is the spectrum of risks presented by automation, especially to well-established organizations. Companies run the risk of dehumanizing and becoming identical to others in their industry—losing whatever their distinctive edge might be and commoditizing themselves in the process. Furthermore, the more we choose to embed all that we do in software, the easier it becomes for competitors to replicate our offering and go a step further at a slightly lower price, locking us into deadly race to the bottom on prices, revenues, and profitability.

What Differentiates Humans from Machines? – The challenge is to harness AI and other disruptive technologies like the Internet of things (IoT) as power tools to support and unleash human potential. At least for some time to come, what differentiates a company will be very human characteristics: The quality of its ideas, strategies, and business models; its community relations; the ability to spot and exploit opportunities or address changing situations, problems, and risks quickly; handling exceptional customer needs; creating new products and services; building deep connections within and outside the organization; how it navigates external developments such as regulatory requirements; and how well it manages change.

These remain very human traits which machines cannot yet replicate. New technologies can play a powerful role in supporting the people performing these tasks and automating the more routine work to free up time for us to undertake these higher level human functions. Organizations that see AI as simply a way to cut back on staffing are missing the point and potentially short-changing their future.

Unleashing Human Potential – Artificial intelligence is increasing business productivity, knowledge, and efficiency, but humans cannot be written off just yet. For example, in the insurance industry, whilst chatbots are emerging at the customer interface, there is a concern that AI is not yet at the point where machines can respond appropriately to distressed customers, an unfortunately common emotional state due to the nature of the matters insurance companies deal with. Artificial intelligence offers a chance to re-humanize the workforce by providing more time to use our talents, softer skills, and emotional intelligence while offloading less sensitive tasks to machines. Obviously, we will need training and support to help us step into these intellectually more demanding roles and to develop our capacity for empathy, sensitivity, compassion, creativity, and intuitive listening.

Q2: How might the new technologies impact the workplace, and what new job opportunities might arise?

As individuals, managers, leaders, investors, and politicians we crave certainty and predictability. We want the future served up to us on a plate with the timelines, impacts, and solutions clearly defined. Reality is far messier and changes constantly—the only certainties are that: 1) Ignoring the emerging future will store up problems; and, 2) trying to apply yesterday's or today's solutions to future challenges will almost certainly fail. What we do know is that the situation will evolve rapidly as the pace of technology development and adoption quickens and businesses seek to act faster to take advantage of what's on offer and respond to potential competitive threats. A wide range of professions from sales person and school teacher to investment banker, risk assessor, claims analyst, plumber, and bus driver will see technology emerge that can enhance or even replace their roles.

Within five years, it is reasonable to foresee quite significant shifts in the types of jobs available, the skills levels required, and a shortening duration for those roles. On a ten-year timeframe, we could reasonably expect to see widespread automation, a dramatic reduction of the jobs that exist today, and new roles emerging in new firms and existing businesses as they seek to stay competitive. Educationally, a degree could become a minimum entry requirement for 80% or more of all new jobs.

So, what about the messy middle between here and the end of the next decade? In the short term, the picture will be confused. Certain firms and industries will accelerate rapidly towards an "employee light" model. Other sectors will see temporary skills shortages until the processes become more automated and the machines learn to code themselves. In professions ranging from machine learning specialists to quantity surveyors, we can see a near-term skills shortage with supply lagging demand. This represents a relatively short window of opportunity to retrain people for these in-demand roles. However, as the process of automation accelerates, and the way we work evolves over the next 5-10 years, we might see these skill shortages erode and the emergence of very different ways of achieving an outcome.

Within a few years, an autonomous vehicle might automatically fine its driver should they choose to take the wheel while drunk or override the speed limit. The vehicle might also self-insure, sharing the risk across the pool of autonomous cars on the road. These smart cars might also drive themselves to the shop for repairs—carried out by a team of robots and drones. These changes wouldn't so much re-engineer the work of solicitors, courtrooms, garages, and insurance firms; rather the activities, associated tasks, and related jobs might be eliminated completely.

New jobs will arise with the emergence of new activities, businesses, and sectors. Human augmentation will require a range of new skills, possibly combined into hybrid roles that draw on chemistry, biology, electro-mechanical engineering, psychology, and counseling. Highly trained workers will also be required in sectors such as smart materials, 3D/4D printing, autonomous car manufacture, superfast construction, environmental protection and remediation, renewable energy, and care of the elderly.

In insurance, the skills of the next generation risk assessor will need to encompass a wider range of disciplines to handle the new fields of science and technology coming to market. At a more fundamental level, we could see a rise in teacher numbers if countries see education as a priority. In parallel, the opportunities in basic and applied R&D could blossom if nations and firms increase their research investments in search of future growth. We could also see a massive growth in small businesses and mentoring roles as people seek to take control of their own destiny. Finally, the stress associated with job displacement due to technology could result in a growing need both for mental health support for people whilst still in the job and for care in the community for those with mental health issues resulting from the loss of their job.

One of the most important things to keep in mind is that there could be many new definitions of the term "job" in the next 5-20 years. A job today is still a fundamental assumption and organizing principle in most Western nations—even if it is being eroded, governments still plan on that basis. A job today is a means to earn money by achieving a set of given tasks. For some it is more—a calling to fulfill one's purpose and give meaning and structure to our lives. For others, it is a means to an end—be that paying for our next meal or providing the money to realize our materialistic, experiential, or spiritual desires.

So, as work is gradually and then more rapidly automated away, what becomes of the job? What might a job look like ten years from now? Will it still be a "production" role delivering measurable daily outputs, or will a job imply a more creative human activity? Will it still be what people do all day? Conceivably, AI could remove aspects of jobs that tend to be considered "work" while emphasizing the parts of a job that make it a social and enriching activity. Will we have moved to a guaranteed or universal basic income (UBI), with people having the choice over where they spend their time, from being a server in a restaurant to taking part in community building restoration projects? The link between how we spend our time and the income we receive might be broken in less than a decade, meaning people could have more autonomy over how they use their time and energy than ever before.

The technology we adopt today will also allow companies to increase their options in terms of achieving outcomes. While Company A might use AI to reduce the size and budget of their legal department, they might in turn boost their investment in the IT and HR departments to ensure they have the right technological capacities and that the lawyers and others they hire are absolutely the right fit. Company B might implement AI to reduce the number of customer service calls routed to human operators, but they could re-invest the salary savings to hire trainers and facilitators to raise digital literacy, emotional intelligence, critical thinking ability, and communication skills across the firm. New training curricula would require new positions to run the programs, e.g. "Director of Life-long Learning." In this case, a job might be more akin to an education: You would leave it smarter and better prepared than when you arrived.

The technologies coming through will also enable and require new professions, and a raft of new roles might emerge across the globe in every sector as we wrestle with the ethical, legal, and societal implications of machine decision making. For example, as driverless vehicles edge closer to becoming a market reality, we may see the rise of the "autonomous ethicist," specialists who attempt to work out the ethics necessary to program autonomous vehicles. This is going to be a social, moral, ethical, political, economic, and—ultimately—legal minefield. Every country, city, region, regulator, insurer, religion, civil rights group, and car manufacturer will want to contribute to the debate. The goal is to try and establish the rules and assumptions that will underpin the decision making within an autonomous vehicle as it becomes aware that it is about to have an accident.

For example, should a self-driving vehicle prioritize the safety of its passenger, the pedestrian who stepped in front of it, or the pregnant mother on the pavement behind them? Should it put the interests of the taxi owner over those of the driver? How will it make those choices? In making those decisions, will it use facial recognition to identify individuals, and pull our tax records and other public information to work out what our net worth is to society or what our future contribution might be? How will it assess the contribution of a writer/journalist versus a baker, doctor, or actuary? What if it chooses to run down an irreplaceable hundred-year-old tree instead of a human?

In a Hindu village in India, for example, running over a cow to save a passenger might be viewed as the worst possible outcome, and therefore the ethics programmed into the vehicle may prioritize the safety of the sacred animal over that of the human. Our ethicists will have to take account of all these different perspectives in constructing their guidance, and views could vary dramatically even within a country.

Q3: What are the implications for how we lead and manage tomorrow's organizations?

Aside from jobs, bringing AI into the workplace successfully will require new leadership styles. The leaders of AI-powered organizations will face unprecedented challenges that could test their people skills and emotional intelligence. "Warm" and highly relatable individuals might be in demand to offset the extent of "cold" automation within an organization. Of course, this won't be universally true—for some, the ultimate goal is to create the DAO, and so for them the pursuit of automation and a workforce led by "robot overlords" is just a stepping stone to the employee-free business of the future. However, at present, humanity seems to be prevailing to some degree, and total digitization seems unlikely to become a genuine threat for most large global businesses in the near term.

Indeed, in a world where there's a risk of automation, dehumanization, and commoditization proceeding hand in hand, those who put people first could find themselves better positioned to create, innovate, adapt, evolve, stand out, and outperform the market. Hence, leaders could become more important than ever, raising their own digital literacy, investing heavily in people development, and demonstrating the kind of extraordinary leadership required in an ever-evolving landscape. In many ways, the real opportunity is being ready to stand up for the longer term with this investment in people, going against a strong near-term focused, pro-AI trend that prioritizes immediate profits over humanity and future business sustainability.

The emphasis on machines, processes, and structures plays into—and perhaps emanates from—the dominant masculine culture in many firms. In contrast, the pursuit of a unique, distinctive, people-centered brand and culture means there could be a greater need for leading from the feminine, with an emphasis on traits such as empathy, social awareness, sensitivity, and collaborative working. Feminine might be just one word for it, but ultimately it is a perspective that puts people, relationships, and the long-term above efficiency and short-term cost savings.

Q4: What might the implications be for large and mature global companies?

Over the next decade, if things follow the "preferred future" that most nations and businesses are pursuing, the global economy could grow from roughly US$75 trillion in 2016 to around US$120 trillion. More than half of that is likely to come from businesses and sectors that have emerged recently or don't yet exist, and over 80% will almost certainly be from products and services we don't have today. For most, this represents a massive opportunity to innovate and evolve to ensure they maintain or attain a leadership position in their sector. The challenge is to embrace innovation at speed across the company and conduct accelerated experiments with a range of new ideas that could help generate near and long-term opportunities.

So, for example, let us consider the insurance sector as a case study. Technological disruption might mean rethinking the entire approach to designing and developing policies. The speed at which markets, products, and services emerge and evolve means that increasingly we may see a shift to simple collective insurance pools, peer-to-peer, and crowdfunding models where the members of a sector ecosystem (customers and suppliers) effectively self-insure. Equally we could see per second policies where objects such as industrial machinery and domestic power tools are connected via the IoT and only insured when actually in use.

Many new sectors, products, and services are emerging at speed—from driverless cars to self-administered neural stimulation drugs and personal genetic enhancement kits. In practice, no insurance company could keep up using current approaches to identifying opportunities, assessing risks, and defining appropriate coverage solutions. The responsibility will need to be handed to the sector participants to create self-service and customizable products. There will be an opportunity here for firms to become the provider of the platforms for sectors and businesses to design their own tailored insurance solutions. Rather than assume responsibility for product development, insurers could provide the software infrastructure, risk assessment models, and investment management tools, and let the industry participants bear the risk.

Industries will also change, meaning lower risk profiles. Smart farms might mean fewer crop-failures, the IoT could enable smart cities with better hazard prevention, and self-driving cars should theoretically never have accidents and hence the notions of self-owning and self-insuring vehicles becomes a possibility. A range of equally dramatic developments across a range of other sectors could have potentially serious implications for insurance.

Across society, changing lifestyles, potentially lower real-term incomes, and smart tracking technology are all driving growth of the sharing economy and scenarios where ownership is rather obsolete, and most possessions are shared, not owned by one individual. This goes along with the shrinking value of owning something and a shift towards purchasing access to it. Shared items could come insured as part of the deal, thus negating any need for buying individual policies. The risks might be borne by the users and reflected in the price. Again, the opportunity for individual firms might be to become leaders in designing customizable sharing economy policies for customers as diverse as power tool manufacturers and community ownership schemes.

The growing experience economy also creates opportunities. For the developed world and middle classes everywhere, we are at a time in history where experiences are starting to matter more than things—whilst tricky to insure, these products could take a similar form to trip insurance. Infinitely flexible policies could be designed to protect people against bad dates or wasting their time on a movie they didn't enjoy. The payout could vary from a ticket refund through to the cost of counseling and treatment should the experience be truly traumatizing.

To enable these kinds of shifts, firms needs to ensure an effective "innovation architecture" that supports a wide range of creative thought and action across all its employees globally. Key components would include ensuring leadership and management truly understand both the technologies reshaping our world and the associated mindsets that are creating new and disruptive concepts, strategies, business models, products, and services. At the local level, the freedom and capacity to conduct rapid market facing experiments is critical—as is the need to have people across the organization seeking out and connecting with emerging businesses and sectors and their respective associations. These market-focused conversations are critical to understanding how current and future sectors and opportunities might evolve. The goal is to gain early access to what might become important future revenues streams.

Firms might also want to consider following the path being pursued by many large organizations that are creating exponential or 10x growth and improvement programs to identify breakthrough ideas that could deliver step change gains internally and in the marketplace. The key is to let ideas blossom and see which ones create the quickest and/or biggest opportunities to take us into the future.

A final piece of the innovation mix is developing a culture of organizational foresight spread across each department and country. This involves consistently scanning the horizon to identify new and emerging societal, technological, commercial, political, and economic developments, which could impact our current and future markets, products, services, and customers—or the way the firm itself operates. Embedding the importance of foresight and long-term thinking could be critical in ensuring the next 5, 50, or 100 years of existence and success.

Q5: How might emerging technologies impact the future products, services, and business models of these large global players?

Over the next decade, pretty much every major business on the planet will probably evolve into a technology company almost indistinguishable from the likes of IBM or Google in its capabilities. The ability to master new technologies such as AI, blockchain, and the IoT will simply be a ticket to the game. Success lies in the firm's ability to leverage that portfolio of smart technologies to help unleash human potential. Let's look at some of the possibilities—again using insurance as a case study.

Artificial intelligence, particularly when combined with other technologies, offers potentially the largest disruption. Internally the technology could transform literally every process within the business. In the marketplace, embedding AI could create wholly new concepts at the boundaries of current insurance thinking. Imagine the smart building that monitors data from tens of thousands of sensors to predict a failure somewhere in its ecosystem and calls in the appropriate inspection or repair; the smart vehicle that fines the driver for speeding and disables itself if the sensors detect alcohol on our breath; the medical monitoring device that manages drug delivery to ensure a constant flow of medication. The applications are literally limitless: Some may create insurance opportunities, while others may open up possibilities that are currently outside our focus and comfort zone.

Sensors and their associated data are enabling the IoT, which could reorient the relationship we have with our natural and physical environments and a whole range of "smart" objects. As technology becomes increasingly observant of us and more and more human behavior is captured, stored, and analyzed, will our regulators and personal privacy preferences allow monitoring to continue along this path? There are still a lot of uncertainties in this area regarding who owns the data. Does it belong to government, like a public resource? To the people? What new insurance product and service opportunities might arise? What role might social media play in accumulating data related to insurance matters—could analysis of a person's social media habits provide a better method of insurance risk assessment than current approaches?

Blockchain, which is the secure ledger technology underlying cryptocurrencies like Bitcoin, could help determine or prove asset ownership and prevent fraud. Smart and open peer-to-peer technologies like blockchain could increase the transparency of risks and force the development of taxes to cover social risks of future technologies. In this case, is it possible that insurance companies based on inevitable surprises could emerge, highlighting and protecting against the inherent biases in technologies?

With the risk of rising economic inequality, clients may increasingly opt to share more personal data to reduce insurance rates, which might also curb their more unsafe activities and behaviors. However, in the smart city context, this may not be required as AI could take on such a large role in our lives as to advise us 24/7, to the extent that poor decisions are automated away, eliminating the inherent biases to make risk-taking more attractive. Technology can enable more customer-centric solutions such as per day mobile phone insurance while travelling.

The needs for insurance could be reduced through the emergence of "self-repairing assets" that use 4D printed, shape-shifting materials for example. Furthermore, 3D printing could allow the cost of manufactured goods to fall so much that people simply insure fewer assets. Finally, life-extension technology emerging from the marriage of Big Pharma and Silicon Valley could create a demographic, economic, and societal tidal wave. How will insurance companies respond if one future perk of wealth is the ability to buy high-tech drugs that allow lifespans of 120 or more years?

Q6: What characteristics should organizations seek to enhance or develop to ensure they have a very human future?

For organizations to navigate the decades ahead, they need to see themselves as a living, breathing, constantly evolving, and very human organization—designed for and by people. This means a culture that embraces continuous innovation and experimentation on both an incremental and a dramatic scale, and a willingness to pursue exponential improvements. Such a journey requires a highly empathetic, trusting, and nurturing relationship with employees where technology is seen as a means of allowing them the time to be creative, innovative, experimental, and customer-centric. In parallel it means being seen to be supportive of those whose jobs are displaced.

If one was to look at any successful brand in a decade's time, we hope it would stand out as forward thinking, opportunity seeking, risk-aware, and farsighted in service of its customers. We would be commending its capacity to anticipate changing societal needs and risks, and its willingness to adapt and evolve to deliver solutions and surprises that meet the needs of a rapidly changing reality or create new sources of delight for the customer.

- *What are the characteristics that will distinguish the winners amongst large multinationals?*
- *How should firms address the management challenge of the exponential pace of development of disruptive technologies?*
- *What might the notion of "employer of choice" look like in a decade's time?*
- *How might we prepare for the "end of jobs"?*

Morning, Noon, and Night – 15 Ways AI Could Transform Daily Life

By Rohit Talwar, Steve Wells, April Koury, Alexandra Whittington, and Maria Romero

How might artificial intelligence impact daily life from dating to disputes and personal development?

Without a doubt, artificial intelligence (AI) has become the hottest topic in town. A combination of breathless excitement and near-paralyzing fear are driving the debate and countless—often ill-informed—predictions about how the technology will revamp our future lives. While it is far too early in AI's evolution to say where it's going or where we might end up, it is already penetrating our lives. From smartphones and dating sites to web searches and driverless vehicles—AI is becoming part of the fabric of life.

Over the next few years, business, home, and schooling could be completely different with AI on the scene. At its core, AI is software or hardware that learns—and it could become programmed to learn mostly about us, its users. The technology is being applied to learn our habits, our likes, and our relationship patterns. Just as Netflix uses an algorithm to suggest films you might watch, a similar "Lifestyle AI" could help choose your wardrobe, your next meal, your job, and your romantic partner. While it all sounds a bit like science fiction, the capabilities of AI tools and the range of applications are growing exponentially. Indeed, by 2020 AI could be present in some form in everything we do. By 2030, AI is likely to have infiltrated our lives in much the same way as smartphones, the internet, and global travel are now taken for granted. So how might AI change our day-to-day existence? Here are fifteen ways our lives could be different in the future as a result of AI.

1. Better Dating and Partner Selection
From one off dates to life partners, AI could access and evaluate the array of big data being amassed about us every day. The matching algorithms could consider everything about us including our social media activity, communication styles, interests, dislikes, DNA profile, medical records, walking speed, aspirations, and relationship history. The systems would help find the right intellectual, emotional, physical, and spiritual match, maybe even determining how long a marriage is likely to last and advising on whether we should even consider longer term relationships.

2. Anticipating your "Party Sick" Fridays
Some companies are exploring the idea of monitoring employees' social media activities to determine if they may be partying a little too hard tonight and thus likely to call in "sick" tomorrow. Knowing in advance would allow for cover to be arranged—this is of particular interest to customer contact centers which need to maintain certain staffing levels to achieve their service targets. Indeed, employers might even offer staff "party days," where they can accrue extra hours which can then be used to sleep it off the morning after a big night out without it affecting their pay or employment records. The entire set of activities described above could all be conducted by AI with no human intervention.

3. Managing our Mental Health
There is a growing incidence of pre-clinical and clinical level mental

health issues across the developed world. From workplace stress to full breakdowns and a range of other conditions, people are struggling to cope with the pressures of modern life. To help address this, AI tools on our phones and computers could monitor everything from our speech patterns and keyboard strokes, to an array of medical indicators captured through body worn devices and implanted sensors.

From early detection of possible issues to providing background guidance during stressful calls and conversations, AI could help manage our mental health. More advanced systems might go so far as to shut down all functionality of our phone and not re-activate it until we have done some meditation or taken a walk. The system could provide our doctors with regular updates on our condition and call in special medical assistance in emergencies.

4. Making Good Decisions

Our AI could become a sort of conscience, reminding us of right and wrong at every turn. This could work on both the individual level ("Should I lie on this job application?") and at an organizational scale ("Should we rip off this customer?"). Not only might AI be deployed as a form of monitoring or "truth detecting" technology that sets off alarms at the source of any mistruth, but data could also become so ubiquitous and verifiable that it won't pay to lie. Along the same lines, crimes of all kinds could become much more difficult to commit. Indeed, law enforcement could eventually get bored and look for something else to do—possibly investing more time in strengthening community engagement.

5. Wardrobe Management

The in store or "on App" AI mirror could show you what you might look like in different colors and sizes of the same dress and under different lighting conditions, simulating work and leisure settings. Knowing your wardrobe, usage patterns, accessorizing approach, and changing fashion interests, your AI could call ahead to the store to have a range of suitable items waiting for you with a human or robotic personal shopper to assist you. When wracked with doubt over whether to make a purchase, your AI could call in the advice of your friends for trusted instant opinions.

6. Mandatory Personal Growth

The ability of AI to help us understand ourselves and learn could lead to lives filled with learning. The "unexamined life" could become obsolete—it may one day be legally impossible to avoid the constant Big Brother data gathering and feedback about one's daily progress against officially defined or personally set physical, emotional, mental, and spiritual development goals. The absence of such goals or tracking information might indicate antisocial tendencies. Everyone might be expected to make full use of AI to become better students, employees, and friends. The gathering of data to improve one's performance in every area would be viewed as a must-do, otherwise, what's the point of collecting it—or indeed—what's the point of living in an organized society?

7. The End of Solitude

The days when someone could take a few days off the grid and disconnect from everything may be coming to an end. For AI to really know its user, the blanket of visible and hidden data collecting sensors that enshroud us must be on and working everywhere and around-the-clock. While you could be physically alone, your digital footprint could reveal your whereabouts in a microsecond. Privacy issues may arise if terms and conditions are not properly established, and security systems will remain vulnerable to hacking. Even in this scenario, it is very likely that you could still be "allowed" to voluntarily turn off your AI, but that alone would be a red flag that might trigger further and more in-depth scrutiny of your behaviors.

8. Legal Dispute Resolution

Many current cases could be directed away from the courts to be resolved by AI judges. For example, in divorce adjudications, employment tribunals, industrial injury claims, and many customer-supplier disputes, judges today are largely applying standard formulae to determine settlements. With AI, a much larger volume of precedents could be considered in a fraction of a second to find the cases that best resemble the current one. Hence greater consistency could then be achieved across the country in the resolution of similar disputes.

In more severe cases such as robbery, murder, or violent crimes, data could be collected and analyzed from the Internet of things (IoT) array of sensors built into everyday objects such as furniture, clothing, and electronic appliances. If the TV room surveillance camera, the sensors in the sofa, and your mobile phone all say you committed the crime, then AI might be able to resolve the case faster and more cheaply than a traditional court room. A jury might still be involved, but the AI would be providing them with more consistent, up-to-date, and precise guidance than any human could ever hope to achieve.

9. Home Management
Consumer AI will enable wave after wave of automatable functions in the home. When combined with appliances, AI could make housework and household management seamless. AI-powered apps, which allow the oven to communicate with the refrigerator and the pantry robot, would act like home chefs. Furthermore, instant replenishment of food and supplies would mean never running out of anything again. Cleaning could be run on appliance to appliance (A2A) scheduling, which robotic cleaners conduct almost completely independently of humans. One of the advantages would be a reduction in household waste, as AI would aim both for efficient use of all products and to perfect the recycling habits of the consumer. Putting the household in better balance with the ecosystem and releasing humans from housework could deliver major benefits in terms of sustainability, time saving, and less domestic stress—at the cost of constant in-home surveillance.

10. The "More Time" Illusion
With all the assistance that AI could provide at work and home, humans might suddenly find themselves with an abundance of leisure

time. Nevertheless, it seems more likely that new expectations could become set and that new activities would emerge. However, there may need to be a trade-off: Just as the introduction of mobile phones made us all available on the go so we could be more productive and "always on," it also invaded our private and recreational time. Hopefully, the new activity choices would be driven by passion, curiosity, and inspiration rather than productivity.

11. Super Personalization

Previous industrial revolutions have favored mass production over personalization, mainly because of the costs of customization. With the introduction of AI and 3D printing to manufacturing processes, a new generation of adaptable production machinery and control software would lower the cost of delivering more customizable products. Today, Amazon and Google use search algorithms to prioritize the results that they believe best match your digital profile. In future, AI could order a unique cereal that would match your desires and diet requirements for the following two weeks. Adoption of AI could enable individually tailored products and services to replace generalized market segmentations.

12. Community Building

Communities may be better organized since AI could monitor and analyze the "health" of the community—covering everything from environmental indicators through to levels of crime, engagement in public spaces, and discussions on web boards and social media. Community planners could harness the intelligence of AI for optimal planning, ensuring that public works and services are available where and when residents need them. For example, AI mapping might help planners identify and predict faster that an area with a rapidly growing population will soon lack sufficient access to schools, health facilities, libraries, and even a fresh food markets. Community managers might send mobile classrooms, GPs, libraries, and fresh food trucks to those areas, or help reorganize the community to self-provision some of the missing essentials.

13. Environmental Monitoring

Environmental conditions may improve by using AI and sensors connected through the IoT to help monitor the local and even global environment. Sensors may constantly feed AI software that records and analyzes the latest local environmental data on factors such as air and water quality. Based on AI predictions and recommendations, commuters may be redirected to public transport or to use reduced emission roads on certain days. In addition, trees and greenery might be planted in specific areas to reduce soil erosion and decrease potential flooding, while entire cities may be redesigned to lessen overall environmental impact on the planet.

14. Personal Travel Agent

Artificial intelligence could be the brain behind future travel and transport planning. Smart tools might evaluate travel preferences in different circumstances and match them against the travel options available. Should I drive, take an Uber, or the train? Should I fly, and where from and to? What connections do I need to reach my destination? How can I make all my business meetings on Friday and still be home in time for my daughter's school play? What is the greenest and least environmentally impactful route I can take? Having created a bespoke itinerary, the AI could complete the necessary reservations, submitting the personal data required to confirm a booking. Not only would AI manage that process, it may also be at the center of the experience where autonomous vehicles control the journey. Whether car, train, bus, plane, the AI would hopefully keep transport system users safer from accidents—where human error has long been the predominant cause.

15. Education Revolution

For a long time now, the criticism of many primary and secondary education systems around the world has been that they are preparing students to pass examinations and not for the world of work they will be joining; especially a world that is evolving rapidly. Artificial intelligence could replace the technical information delivery role currently undertaken by teachers. The AI system could monitor each student on a range of subjects designed to prepare them for the future world of work. No longer will all students work to the same or similar curriculum through all 11 years of primary and secondary education. Instead they would have a carefully planned and constantly monitored, evolving, and personalized program.

Personal curricula would be designed to stretch and develop each student with the skills he/she needs for the expected types of jobs or further education landscape they might encounter at 16 years of age. Students will still need someone in the classroom, but maybe the human "teacher" is responsible for helping advise on research strategies and problem-solving approaches, encouraging group work and collaboration, nurturing individuals, and providing emotional support. The primary role of teachers would be helping students develop the social and meta-learning skills required to enable each to play a full role in the emerging world—served by the machines—thus ensuring every individual a very human future.

- *How do you see AI most impacting your life?*
- *What new possibilities could open up for you with AI?*
- *What do you hope won't change as AI penetrates every aspect of human activity?*

How Artificial Intelligence Might Help Us Decode Our World

By Rohit Talwar, Steve Wells, April Koury, Maria Romero, and Alexandra Whittington

How might AI enhance the quality of our friendships and relationships?

Popular films like *Her* and TV series such as *Black Mirror* depict a future of intimate relationships in a high-tech world: Man falls in love with operating system, woman loves person she meets in virtual reality. The rise of technologies like artificial intelligence (AI) may play a huge role in the future of our interpersonal relationships. One example of what this AI could look like is hardware that we could touch and feel, such as robots; another would be software, or algorithms that take on a persona like Alexa or Siri and can seemingly interact with us.

Beyond overused sci-fi clichés, there's great potential for AI to increase the authenticity and value of real human relationships. Below are some scenarios of how AI might enhance the quality of friendship, romantic, and professional relationships.

Dating

Men are from Mars and women are from Venus, but AI can be

programmed to translate, helping circumvent missteps in love. Algorithms—as key matchmakers in the future of dating—might provide the support and information people need to extend the connection beyond the first date. For example, an AI personal assistant may give insights on how to approach someone for a second date based on information culled from the first meeting, the internet, and various digital databases. Soon, one's tweets, Facebook "likes," and circle of friends could be used to build our dating profile and then compile a fool-proof user guide to dating the other person.

Imagine a Netflix for dates, informing you of the right restaurants to suggest for a certain someone based on their biological profiles, DNA tests, or other obtainable digital data about them. How about narrowing down your choice of bars and cafes based on the probability of meeting singles with a certain Myers-Briggs profile? Whilst on a date, our AI assistant could be interpreting micro-facial expressions and suggesting underlying meanings and desires in what the other person is saying. The technology could also relay real-time video to our inner circle of friends—collating and prioritizing advice from them and dating guides across the web. We need never be lost for words or misinterpret a cue again.

Family

Robots used in caring for the elderly is a no-brainer in places like Japan where the population is aging rapidly and there is a shortage of caregivers. However, it is possible that AI will one day help us communicate and relate better with our elderly friends, relatives, and neighbors. Hearing and speech enhancement is a major area that AI will impact—in fact, teaching robots to listen and respond to human speech is an essential aspect of moving AI into our homes and workplaces. Facial recognition and reading body language are among some of the cutting-edge capabilities of AI that could enhance elder care.

It is possible that future AI programs will help us not just care for the older people in our lives in a superficial way; today we are familiar with the ability to harness technology for medication reminders, virtual doctor visits, and obtaining information used for at-home care. In the near future, AI might keep older people company in the absence of a caring adult, or help caregivers understand illness and injury with more empathy. In a more distant future, the ability to upload memories to the cloud could make the impacts of Alzheimer's obsolete—AI could help patients recall past events and make sense of the present. Combined with virtual reality and augmented reality, we may reach breakthroughs with AI when it comes to understanding the aging experience and avoiding its pitfalls, such as loneliness, communication problems, and memory loss.

Friendships

In the age of social media, one can have hundreds of online connections with no real friends in sight in the "real world." Loneliness is an epidemic, and surveys have reported that people believe the number of flesh-and-blood "friends" they can count on in times of need is decreasing compared to past samples. Technology does not have to alienate us from each other, though, hence the growing societal emphasis on the role of technology in enhancing humanity, not diminishing it.

So how could AI help us in our friendships? First of all, guarding special relationships takes tact and care that can be difficult for some people and at certain times during life. Various uses of AI, like voice detection, could help us learn how to treat a friend who calls to casually "say hi," but whose voice holds fear or anxiety undetectable to the human ear. Friendships might be less private, but more authentic with such a technology. On the other hand, the art of the "little white lie" could be perfected by some device which could let us know when bending the truth might preserve a relationship. Conversely, how many friendships would survive a lie detector test enabled on every conversation?

Career

Could AI help you ask for a raise one day? It's possible our digital twins, our futuristic personal assistants that mirror our thoughts, actions, and activities, might make appropriate suggestions along our career paths which help us get ahead. Digital twins might look out for us by comparing salary data in our fields, for example, providing both moral and evidential support to the big ask. Furthermore, AI-powered services could suggest, provide, and track professional development training to help instill confidence and overcome weaknesses.

As a job coach, AI might provide valuable assistance to job seekers as well as support people on the job to maintain credentials. Competition in the job market will be fierce once automation takes hold of a range of white-collar jobs. Artificial intelligence working to advance humanity in the workplace would be a win-win for organizations and employees alike. Career support is one application for technology that would enhance the human role in the workplace, while positioning AI in a manner which is not overpowering or threatening.

Ultimately the role of AI in the future of society is still to be determined. Whilst futurists and other early adopters are busy talking up the benefits of AI, new risks are exposed every day. For example, self-driving cars could reduce the number of lives lost in car accidents, and force repair garages and auto insurance firms to find a new purpose or go out of business. Algorithms that can predict start-up success rates are handy, but could they ultimately quash innovation? It's fascinating to see the artwork created by a robot, but what about human creativity—and preserving those qualities that make us human? Given the profit motive, AI is already out of the bag. But how we use it and whether it is harnessed to enhance human potential are ultimately choices that we as humans have to make.

- *What unexpected consequences could emerge from the application of AI to dating and relationships?*
- *How might the nature of family dynamics change with AI?*
- *Could AI level the playing field in the workplace if everyone is using it for career advice?*

A version of this article was originally published in *Guru & Go*

The Human, Smart, and Sustainable Future of Cities

By Rohit Talwar, Steve Wells, April Koury, Alexandra Whittington,
and Maria Romero

How might future cities best reflect our prevailing social and economic
priorities and take advantage of technological possibilities?

The city of the future is a symbol of progress. The sci-fi vision of the future city with sleek skyscrapers and flying cars, however, has given way to a more plausible, human, practical, and green vision of tomorrow's smart city. Whilst smart city visions differ, at their heart is the notion that, in the coming decades, the planet's most heavily concentrated populations will occupy city environments where a digital blanket of sensors, devices, and cloud-connected data is weaved together to build and enhance the city living experience for all. In this context, smart architecture must encompass all the key elements of what enable city ecosystems to function effectively. This means everything from the design of infrastructure, workspaces, leisure, retail, and domestic homes to traffic control, environmental protection, and the management of energy, sanitation, healthcare, security, and a building's eco-footprint.

The world's premier cities and architects are competing to design and build highly interconnected smart environments where people, government, and business operate in symbiosis with spectacular, exponentially improving array of technologies from artificial intelligence (AI) to renewable energy and the Internet of things (IoT). The architectural promise of future smart cities is to harmonize the benefits of these disruptive technologies for society and provide a high quality of life "by design." Some have already implemented smart city architecture and, as the concepts, experiences, and success stories spread, the pursuit of "smart" will become a key driver in the evolving future of cities as communities and economic centers. Here we explore some of the critical trends, visions, ideas, and disruptions shaping the rise of smart cities and smart architecture.

Smart Cities - Purpose, Engagement, and Vision

The evidence to date from smart city and smart architecture initiatives around the world is that the best results come when we have a clear sense of what the end goal is. However, in a fast changing world, it can be hard to develop a clear future vision and strategy when stakeholder goals are not aligned, where every sector is being disrupted, and all our planning assumptions are being challenged. A city vision might take 5-15 years to roll out—but for many businesses and individuals it is almost impossible to think about their needs 24 months from now. However, the challenge must be overcome.

City governments have to work together with architects to create inclusive processes that inform citizens about the forces shaping the future and the possibilities on the horizon. The next step is to engage the population in dialogue concerning the kind of future city we want to create. We have to explore what a livable city means to its people and be clear on how we will design and build the structures to support that vision. Alongside this, we need to articulate a clear vision and direction around education, environment, public services, access to justice, city administration, and civic engagement. These pillars then provide the guiding requirements which will, in turn, influence the design of the physical, digital, and human elements of the infrastructure and building architectures that enable a smart city.

Big Data: Smart Architecture to Power a City

Smart cities are designed to inform decisions by capturing massive amounts of data about the population and its patterns, such as water use and traffic flows. This information gathering results in big data, which is essentially gathered via different forms of surveillance. The ease and affordability of cameras, sensors, AI, and advanced analytics in the future will mean this data gathering function may become completely automated. Indeed, the data will be collated from a constantly evolving and expanding IoT, encompassing traffic lights and cameras, pollution sensors, building control systems, and personal devices—all literally feeding giant data stores held in the cloud. The ability to crunch all this data is becoming easier due to rampant growth in the use of predictive algorithms and AI application software that run on networks of high performance computing and storage devices.

Singapore is a leading example of a smart city, and is constantly evolving its "city brain," a backbone of technologies used to help control pollution, monitor traffic, allocate parking, communicate with citizens, and even issue traffic fines. Singapore's "brain" is also attempting to modify human behavior. For example, one system rewards drivers for using recommended mapped routes, and punishes those who do not. Now imagine expanding this use of big data to human foot traffic around and within the buildings of a city. For some time now, companies like Pavegen and Veranu have been developing flooring that harvests the energy of walking and converts it into electricity. By analyzing foot traffic patterns, smart architects may be able to design entire buildings powered solely by their inhabitants' movements.

Internet of Things: Redesigning Spaces

Smart cities rely on advanced technology to make sense of massive arrays of data. Indeed, the amount of information on the internet is expected to grow exponentially as a result of the Internet of things. Essentially IoT means that everything ("things")—and potentially everyone—will form a network of beacons and collection devices, gathering data on ambient and behavioral patterns from our surroundings, feeding this information to the city brain in the cloud.

Hence, after data, the IoT is the second driving force behind the rise of smart infrastructure: For everything from air conditioning to parking meters to function effectively and seamlessly in a smart city, microphones, sensors, voice recognition, and all sorts of other high-tech gadgetry must be hooked up to the IoT.

Architects and planners are already exploring the possibilities—indeed, technology players like IBM, Hitachi, and Cisco are all betting big on IoT-enabled smart buildings. Exhaustive monitoring of internal building conditions offers the potential to provide future occupants with seamlessly and continuously optimized living conditions while reducing energy and space wastage. Today's smart sensors can recognize occupancy patterns and movement to switch on the air conditioning or lights for a person before they even enter a room, and shut off these systems as they exit. The more we know about the specific individuals, the more we can tailor those setting to their personal preferences.

In the near future, buildings will potentially be built on a smart IoT grid that monitors, controls, and automates smart lighting and intuitive heating, ventilation, and air conditioning to create the perfect environment while drastically decreasing energy wastage. Furthermore, IoT devices combined with big data analysis may help architects redesign and readapt buildings to minimize energy wastage, and maximize space usage, both shrinking resources in our ever-growing cities. Single use facilities like meeting rooms—traditionally unused for periods of time—may be redesigned as multipurpose spaces that support a whole host of day-to-day business activities based on analyses of data gathered via the IoT. A smart building may even take on the management of meeting rooms to sell vacant space to third party users on a per minute basis: For example, a row of meeting rooms by day could become a nightly pop-up market.

Sustainability: Smart Building Materials

Finally, from an architectural design perspective, all this data and awareness should enable decisions that make the best possible use of material resources with an emphasis on sustainability. This is a very logical outcome and benefit of the merging of big data, AI, and the IoT feeding into the rise of smart architecture.

Given that the UK has recently broken energy use records with solar meeting almost a quarter of energy demands, there is significant potential for the sun to become a mainstream power source in current and future building designs. There is also a new scientific forecasting tool to predict solar weather, which will make the rollout of solar on buildings (and in homes) a more feasible option. Eventually, with a growing array of such distributed power solutions, a centralized energy distribution grid for homes and businesses may not be necessary.

Additionally, the exponential growth in, and reduced cost of, solar technology may lead to entire cities designed to generate their own electricity. Rather than glass windows, skyscrapers could be covered in transparent solar panels that, through IoT monitoring, turn slightly opaque as the sun moves over them throughout the day. This would allow the darker panels to not only gather more energy, but also shade the building's inhabitants and decrease cooling costs. Researchers at RMIT University in Australia are currently working on a solar paint that absorbs moisture from the air and turns it into hydrogen fuel, one of the cleanest sources of energy available. Soon, architects may begin designing buildings based around maximizing the benefits of these next generation "smart" materials.

Cities Get Smart

The smart city movement has the potential to transform the organization of people, materials, and physical objects in a way that transcends urban development as we know it. The shift to smart architecture is not simply fashionable or aspirational; in many ways, it appears to be a critical enabler of the future sustainability of cities. It can be argued that the future of human life on the planet rests on a smooth transition to cities that are more efficient, less wasteful, and more conscious of the impacts of the individual upon the greater good.

It is now possible to create and deliver a city vision with citizens at its heart, and that is enabled by forward thinking infrastructure coupled with judicious use of enabling technologies. A well thought through vision, enabled by robust and well-executed smart architecture, could provide a foundation stone for the next stage of our development, where science and technology are genuinely harnessed in service of creating a very human future.

- *Which social values would help ensure a very human vision of tomorrow's smart city?*
- *How can we encourage people, businesses, and governments to create human-centered cities?*
- *What are the critical infrastructure elements required to enable a smart city?*

A version of this article was originally published in *E-architect* under the title "Human, Smart and Sustainable Future of Cities."

IMPACTS OF AI
ON MAJOR INDUSTRIES

AI and Healthcare - The Now, The Next, and The Possible

The Creative and Destructive Impacts of AI-Powered FinTech on Financial Services

Riding Shotgun with Autonomous Vehicles

Robo-Retail vs. Humanity at a Price? Two Possible Futures for Retail

Unleashing the True Potential of AI - Building the Exponential Law Firm

A Day in the Life of a Legal Project Manager: June 1st, 2020

Most Exponential Law Firms 2025

Artificial Intelligence and the Growth Opportunity for Accounting Firms

Designing for a Post-Job Future: The Impact of AI on Architecture

AI and the Many Possible Futures of the IT Professional

Artificial Intelligence - The Next Frontier in IT Security?

AI and Healthcare – The Now, The Next, and The Possible

By Rohit Talwar, Steve Wells, and Katharine Barnett

What might a plausible timeline of artificial intelligence developments in the healthcare industry look like over the short, medium, and longer term?

Artificial intelligence (AI) has reached a level of capability and maturity where it could have a transformative impact on healthcare and other knowledge intensive sectors. The power, scope, and scale of AI applications are increasing exponentially. Here, we explore the current uses, emerging applications, and future possible impact of AI in healthcare. Finally, to offer a glimpse of the sheer scale of what is over the horizon, we present a scenario outlining the revolutionary impact AI could have on the central tenets and functioning of the UK healthcare system—although many of the ideas would have global applicability.

Technological Disruption

The technological revolution is already disrupting the healthcare industry across the globe. Incredible developments in the power and precision of new and emerging technologies are driving radical changes in diagnosis, drug development, treatment plans, surgery techniques, monitoring devices, estates, and facility management. Already, there are remote patient monitoring devices that feed back their readings in real time; blood pressure, glucose levels, heart rates, and more can all be tracked. Sub-miniature electronics has given rise to "lab-on-a-chip" diagnostic tools—only a few square millimeters in size—that can replicate many of the functions of an entire laboratory.

What's next?

Exponentially accelerating advances in science and technology are now taking us to the next level and blurring the boundaries between science fiction and reality. For example, with a wry eye to the future, Qualcomm offered a US$10 million X-prize for the invention that best replicates the Star Trek Tricorder medical instrument, the small hand-held device that can diagnose all illnesses. With only a slight scaling back on the functionality of the Star Trek solution, Qualcomm challenged their entrants to diagnose over a dozen medical conditions. The winning submissions were announced in the second quarter of 2017 with Final Frontier Medical Devices and Dynamical Biomarkers Group winning first and second prizes for their solutions.

In this era of groundbreaking technological innovations, special attention should be paid to the revolutionary developments enabled and promised by AI. Some are calling it mankind's last invention because of its potential to reach a super intelligent status that far exceeds human capabilities. While that ultimate invention may be some way off, right now AI has the potential to disrupt the healthcare industry from the inside; to become embedded in every aspect of healthcare provision, bringing about monumental changes for patient and provider alike.

Artificial Intelligence

Currently the power and scale of AI technology is starting to drive significant developments within the healthcare sector. Already, AI is being used for diagnosis and prediction, drug development, healthcare management—applications that are improving efficiency and cutting costs. As outlined in a previous article, we are already seeing staggering results in the use of AI technology in medical diagnosis and prediction. For example, the IBM Watson Health application can process, analyze, and extrapolate inferences from huge amounts of data, and is already outperforming cancer experts in patient diagnosis.

In another development, Google DeepMind has launched Deep-Mind Health: In a five-year deal with the UK's National Health Service (NHS), the company will access NHS patient data to help develop and deploy its Streams healthcare app. This app will alert healthcare professionals to patients in most need, will allow them to securely assign tasks, and communicate about workload decisions. It aims to provide mobile viewing of results, patient medical histories, and messaging; the alerts should speed up delivery of care and the hope is that the application will revolutionize the outdated model of task allocation by paper memos and fax machines. These are examples of what's happening now—so what else can we expect?

What's on the horizon?

Predictive Diagnosis
The rapidly increasing processing power and functionality of health-care AI applications will enable huge amounts of data from multiple sources to be aggregated, analyzed, and extrapolated, allowing ever more sophisticated and comprehensive insights, inferences, and causal patterns to be identified. This underlying process may, in the very near future, change diagnosis and guide all subsequent patient interactions throughout the treatment process. These applications can draw input from a far more diverse range of sources that most humans would have the time, inclination—and possibly the capacity—to gather, analyze, and interpret. For example, data can be combined from wearable devices, healthcare records, genetic information, family histories, food diaries, shopping purchases, patient income statements, public health sources, and local authority databases.

By using a wide array of relevant information in a predictive and pre-emptive manner, we may be able to eradicate the notion of diagnosis as clinical practice that only takes place once symptoms have manifested. Instead, the predictive power of AI could be applied to these data sets to assess or predict the likelihood of conditions, diseases, or illnesses that a patient might develop in coming years. This hyper-early prediction will allow sufficient time for interventions to take place, and with increasing success. Lifestyles can be altered, prophylaxis administered, and special attention paid to the manifestation of indicative symptoms, enabling treatment to be initiated immediately if a health risk does indeed become apparent. This should deliver significantly better patient outcomes, and lower rates of admission to secondary care will put fewer burdens on health system budgets.

Patient Pathway Management

Enhanced patient pathway management is another key AI development we may see in the near future, which will have particular resonance in the UK from both a patient care and a funding perspective. The UK NHS is split into Clinical Commissioning Groups (CCGs), clinically led statutory bodies responsible for the planning and delivery of healthcare within their local area. As patients and their records transition through the healthcare system, there is the potential for administrative errors and issues. To help address this, an AI embedded in a patient's smart device can use data collected from multiple sources: Patient records, interactions, social media, and transactions can all be aggregated and processed to draw out potential patient behaviors.

In this scenario, AI systems would alert patients to take their medications, turn up to appointments, and provide them with information. This will be radically different from the current text update service that the NHS provides. Instead of a standard text to remind patients of appointment times, these nudges will be unique, personalized to the individual, use language they are accustomed to, and present information in a format that will be most easily understandable to that individual. In the near future, we may see this evolve from a text message to a GIF, image, or animation that appears on a young person's phone reminding them of their appointment. Equally, a robot generated voice memo might be sent to a lawyer to remind them to take their medication, which they can listen to in between seeing clients.

Alongside helping the individual take action, the AI could also manage their time and appointments without them ever knowing. If a consultation needs to be booked and a patient allows access to the ever-smarter intelligent assistants (e.g., future generations of Siri) on their smartphones, then the AI could look at the patient's calendar and upcoming commitments, extrapolate data from their movements and lifestyle choices, and book a convenient appointment time. So, knowing a particular student habitually misses morning classes, the AI would schedule an afternoon consultation. Similarly, a parent who works part time can automatically have their appointments booked for mid-morning after the school run. There will be no need to enter this information; the AI will "know" it from the deep inferences drawn from data analysis.

Such AI enabled applications in early diagnosis and patient management systems could radically improve outcomes, increase efficiency, and cut costs significantly. The savings could be directed to more labor-intensive practices such as surgery and to funding critical research projects. Early successes with clear benefits from the adoption of AI applications could lead to a rapid and potentially exponential increase in the usage, reach, scope, and impact of such smart tools across the health service.

Future Innovation – Radical Convergence

Looking slightly further into the future, we may see AI embedded in all aspects of the process. For example, significant change could come by linking AI to blockchain technology. Blockchain is a form of distributed ledger technology that is used to provide a super secure, time stamped immutable "block" or record for each transaction, which includes information from the previous record in the chain. This means transactions cannot be deleted or amended. Originally developed to record transactions undertaken in the Bitcoin cryptocurrency, increasingly applications are being seen in tasks like transaction tracking in financial services. The combined application of AI and blockchain could radically alter the flow of funds through the entire healthcare system.

The existing UK funding system lacks the flexibility and sufficiently sophisticated technology solutions to allow for the concept of having the money actually following the patient throughout the system. In contrast, as the AI is planning pathways, directing patients, and guiding medical intervention, the transactions and interactions could be tracked and time stamped using a blockchain.

The use of blockchain will provide an immutable healthcare transaction record, allowing for instant identification of the funds available and the amount spent on a particular patient. So, this system would offer the seemingly impossible and revolutionary benefit of tracking both the cost of each intervention and—possibly—the value of its outcome. With the record that blockchain offers, the impact of each individual intervention could be tracked across the whole of the healthcare system thereafter. This would provide a concrete basis for a system of value-based pricing to be implemented; the value being drawn out of an assessment of the balance between the total cost and resources used for an intervention and the resulting increase of healthy years of life as an outcome.

The Furthest Reaches of AI

On a 10 to 20-year horizon, it is possible that AI could actually protect us from any knowledge of our condition, allowing us to go about our daily lives blissfully unaware of all the technological magic that is happening behind the scenes to help us stay fit, healthy, and happy. The emerging applications explored above—hyper-early diagnosis, smart management of patient pathways, coordination between departments, guidance through consultations, and alerts to take medication—can all be done with minimal knowledge on the part of the patient. So, in the first generation of such systems, patients could sign a digital consent form, stating the different levels of knowledge they would like.

For some patients who see healthcare worries as an undue burden on their lives, they may agree to receive no factual information on their condition at all. Alerts may read something like "We have booked you an appointment with your doctor to receive some medication that may be beneficial to you." To reduce stress and, in turn, maximize outcomes, each stage of their treatment could be conducted using friendly, neutral, or disinterested language depending on the patient's preference and what the system has learnt from past interactions.

For those less worried—or perhaps intrigued—by their potential medical conditions, more direct language could be used. They could be informed of the biological processes that may occur, told what symptoms may arise, what to expect, and when to expect it. Some may prefer to go further and receive in-depth biomedical information, review charts tracking their progress, see other patient group statistics, be offered links to useful website, and view videos of procedures—all as selectable options to be included in their guidance and support package.

In the second-generation version, patients would have no need to even sign a consent form. The AI would have learned about the patient by gleaning data and insight from multiple sources, and simply "know" what information it would be necessary for each person to be made aware of, and when to provide it. The system could determine salient personality traits from your data and interactions to discern who should be told what, when, and how much. It will also be able to differentiate when—if you are usually a highly inquisitive and stable individual—a recent high intensity workload has induced a stressful period in your life. The AI will recognize this from analyzing your information and interacting with your intelligent assistant behind the scenes, and tailor its interactions with you to ensure minimal stress and maximum efficiency.

Going a step further, it is possible that an AI will be able to build an effective medicine regime, tailoring the size and timing of dosage to have maximum effect given your personal physiology. By analyzing your treatment responses and condition changes over time, it could start to make decisions about adapting or completely changing your medication regime. The AI could send information directly to a regional pharmacy, where complex multi-drug ingredients would be combined in 3D printed multi-pills. Using all the data about an individual, including their unique genetic code, these drugs would be designed specifically for each patient. We can anticipate that with a convergence of applications and technologies, the AI could take over many such aspects of healthcare delivery.

The Revolution is Underway

While we are at the very early stages of the adoption of AI in healthcare, the take up is likely to accelerate—driven by the proven benefits of AI technology and its potential to improve outcomes, increase efficient use of scarce resources, and drive down the cost of delivering care. As we look to the future, an increasingly sophisticated range of AI applications promise to deliver timely and completely individualized medical intervention with minimal resource wastage and to potentially revolutionize the funding structure of our healthcare systems. This could herald a new age of intelligent care, one that takes a holistic view of every aspect of a human and directs advice, action, and intervention to help ensure their total well-being. The ultimate goal here is not to become subservient to the machine, but rather to harness its immense potential in service of humanity.

- *What ethical issues could emerge from AI keeping personal data hidden from its owner?*
- *What new skills will doctors, nurses, and other healthcare professionals require in order to adapt to these revolutionary changes?*
- *How can we build trustworthy relationships with patients so they embrace the use of AI in healthcare?*

A version of this article was originally published in *HefMa Pulse*.

The Creative and Destructive Impacts of AI-Powered FinTech on Financial Services

By Rohit Talwar, Steve Wells, and Alexandra Whittington

How might artificial intelligence impact the jobs landscape in the financial sector?

Of all the business technologies that have come to market recently, artificial intelligence (AI) has been the one generating the most buzz, expectation, and hype. It is also spawning an ever-growing set of doom-laden predictions of how it could be society's last big invention and bring about the end of jobs as we know them in industries such as financial services. The simple truth is that we are at a very early stage in the evolution of AI and its disruptive technology cousins. As a result, no one knows for sure the likely scale of activity automation and job losses or, conversely, the amount of opportunities that could be created by AI—either within existing businesses or in the new sectors and firms that are emerging. To help explore the possibilities, here we examine some of the ways in which AI could impact financial services and enable new FinTech ventures, particularly regarding robo-investment and chatbots.

Part of the reason that interest, experimentation, and adoption of AI is accelerating is that major "cloud services" providers such as Amazon, Google, and Salesforce, are making relatively low-cost AI services available to firms of every size. This enables customers to apply sophisticated machine learning-based AI tools to the manipulation of very large datasets, providing a real boost to start-ups and smaller firms that would not normally have the R&D resources to develop such applications on their own. This sort of AI as a Service model is spawning several start-ups–especially in the FinTech space– and enhancing the offerings of already-established companies. The overall effect is to raise the capability, reach, and competitiveness for all small- and medium-sized businesses.

The financial sector examples below should help illustrate which particular jobs or tasks AI would handle easily, and highlight the new opportunities that could arise once humans are freed from those tasks. We find it balances the discussion a little to put some attention on the possible positive developments that could also unfold, including the creation of entirely new jobs.

Robo-Investment

At the moment, the investment sector is anticipating widespread replacement of humans by bots and algorithms—and with good reason. Many current sector roles focus largely on numerical analysis of trends and performance charts, a task which AI can perform more rapidly, comprehensively, and reliably than most humans. In recent months we've seen Blackrock, the world's largest asset manager, announce that 50% of its human fund managers are underperforming the market trackers, and that it is undertaking a program of replacing them with AI-based algorithms. A range of AI fund management tools have also come to market recently. For example, numerai is a crowd-sourced investment tool with over 7,000 data scientists contributing to its development. LendingRobot is an AI algorithm-managed hedge fund that invests in lending marketplaces, charges fees significantly lower than other human-managed funds, and does all its reporting via blockchain.

In future, it's possible that AI investment tools will predict interest rates, currency movements, and other economic indicators. For example, the advisory firm PwC has developed an algorithm with

92% accuracy in predicting national GDP. Rapid advances in the ability of AI to crunch massive amounts of financial data make its application to investment processes a no-brainer. The rapid automation of finance means that analysts, traders, brokers, advisors, and even personal bankers could at least partially be replaced by the technology.

But it is shortsighted to just think of job losses. Most current AI-based tools are learning their craft from humans, so the latter will still be required to deal with new situations and more complex requirements. We also think the technology frees people up from the "dishwashing"—i.e. routine and mundane tasks—to focus on the more creative challenges of customer engagement, designing new products and services, crafting solutions to complex internal and client challenges, scanning for what's next, and doing genuinely game changing thinking. Clearly, realigning staff to these new roles will require individual and corporate investment in training and personal development to ensure the desired mind shift and capability building take place.

At the same time, emerging AI-powered FinTech concepts have tremendous potential to create entirely new and interesting roles and occupations. For example, banks have massive amounts of consumer spending, savings, and investment data to feed into AI algorithms; however, delivering value to clients will require humans with financial literacy, new expertise, and insights which could become the foundation for customer seminars and personalized financial planning services. This could represent a return to more traditional roles for the local bank manager.

New services and business models might be generated from the large amount of information that proprietary algorithms would make available cheaply and easily. Relationships with customers can be given priority in this scenario, which would also require new job roles and capabilities, such as people skills and emotional intelligence, not to mention coding to build the algorithms. Finance employees working alongside AI could evolve into roles that are primarily creative, educational, and supportive—which seems like a very human complement to an otherwise highly automated experience.

New players entering the FinTech scene have the blessing of zero legacy to deal with. Hence, they can start from the outset by focusing on their end-customers and designing solutions entirely tailored to their needs, be that investment, transactions, or insurance. An example would be Monzo, a constantly evolving personal finance app built entirely around the way some segments of society now lead their lives. In such cases, humans are still generally far better suited than AI software for tasks like understanding potential customers, co-creating solution concepts, prototyping, and ultimately building and refining the resulting services. In addition, new players have to build alliances, raise finance, market themselves, develop social media buzz, prove their capabilities to would-be partners and customers, and deliver ultra-fast service responses. Again, in a relationship-driven world, these are all roles for which humans will still have the edge for some time to come.

Chatbots

Already several banks such as Royal Bank of Scotland, Swedbank, Bank of America, and Capital One are using customer-facing bots to take requests, answer simple questions, and perform basic tasks via mobile devices, Facebook, and other platforms like Amazon Alexa. These service offerings are extending in scope and functionality. For example, messaging app Kik is releasing its own cryptocurrency tokens as a digital currency similar to Bitcoin for use within its platform. Called Kin, the cryptocurrency can presently be spent in interactions with a chatbot to buy services and products on Kik. In the future, users could also engage in peer-to-peer commerce using Kin. Such apps suggest that routine banking roles of teller, service agent, loan officer, and supervisor could all be considered ripe for automation or elimination.

Indeed, AI already lends itself well to roles requiring high volume data processing, consistency, and attention to detail. So, what new roles might emerge? For example, rather than view the human-staffed bank as doomed, it might be more inspiring to think of it as a future messaging app or social media site; rather than fire entire labor pools and replace them with robots, banks could flip the model and turn branches into "experience and learning centers." Here staff would facilitate conversations to help customers solve problems together, connect with each other, and design new products. They could transition veteran workers into roles focused on development of meaningful experiences to touch on the day-to-day lives of customers—for example, helping them learn how to use tools such as new FinTech applications, messaging apps like Kik, and social media platforms like Facebook.

Some displaced workers might find alternative livelihoods working for the FinTechs or participating in projects such as Kin. For example, current uses of Kin include tipping others for making outstandingly good posts or shares on the platform—humor, for example, is rewarded. This might be the kind of activity that could replace a "job" in the future, with income gained via performance on social media or in virtual communities of some kind, paid in cryptocurrency.

The Post-Job Future

Companies that simply slash workforces in the name of efficiency without exploring the bigger picture could be throwing out the baby with the bathwater. The risk is that entirely automated organizations will become undifferentiated and commoditized without human ingenuity to drive constant innovation. Automation of jobs provides an opportunity to tap a vast pool of employee experience for meaningful value in the quest to develop new services and products. Veteran financial workers could be viewed as an important source of knowledge of what working in a bank is really like, and what true customer needs are. A robot can post deposits and certify documents quickly and consistently; however, designing, building, and training an in-branch chatbot is a job best carried out currently with human input. Complementing AI investment tools with behavioral and motivational advice from suitably trained staff could help customers increase their returns, generate higher profits for the banks, and create new opportunities for those with different skillsets.

It is important to acknowledge the reality of workplace automation: Experts predict up to 50% of all jobs (or more) could disappear by 2035, while others suggest that only 5% might disappear while 65% could be affected materially. However, it is much harder to predict the extent to which they will be replaced by roles that have not yet been invented, in firms yet to be born, in industries that are only just emerging. As we said at the start, predicting the outcome is nigh on impossible this early in the game. That AI will impart both creative and destructive effects is a fact of the coming technology revolution that can give us hope and guide more human-centered decisions. The key is to start acting now to train employees with new skills and start creating the new, more customer-oriented and creative roles in anticipation of relatively rapid changes on the horizon.

- *How can we capitalize on the changes AI and FinTech might bring to the relationship between financial service providers and customers?*
- *How can we harness and nurture the wisdom of veteran employees?*
- *Could AI help technology companies take over the financial industry, or might it help financial service companies to consolidate their position?*

A version of this article was originally published in *Small Business* under the title "How AI enabled financial services and FinTech are taking jobs."

Riding Shotgun with Autonomous Vehicles

By Rohit Talwar and Alexandra Whittington

How might autonomous vehicles transform the automotive aftermarket, cities, and societies?

Bold predictions and skeptical challenges abound regarding the speed with which autonomous vehicles could emerge. The evangelists believe we could see a rapid evolution from "level 1" function specific automation of tasks—such as stability control—through to "level 4" fully self-driving vehicles. Indeed, in early 2017 Elon Musk, the founder of Tesla, claimed that full autonomy could be less than six months away. Whilst that prediction didn't materialize and development to date has been relatively slow (as with most current fields of technology), we are likely to see a rapid, if not exponential, acceleration of the self-driving sector. Hence, for the vehicle recovery and repair sector, now is the time to start thinking about the potential evolution of autonomous cars and the resulting implications and opportunities.

Dramatic claims are being made about the potential for autonomous vehicles to cut accident rates, reduce the need for vehicle repairs drastically, improve fuel management, increase traffic flows, and lower the number of taxis required in a city. This could transform the automotive sector, enhance the productivity of human "drivers," make car journeys fun again, render cities more livable, and reinvent auto insurance. Here, we look at where some of these claims stand,

and bring a futurist's professional perspective to assess the cultural and consumer shifts that could arise from a move toward self-driving cars.

Accident Rates

An op-ed written by Barack Obama in 2016 cited the fact that 94% of car accident deaths are caused by human error. Making driving safer is a key assumption when it comes to promoting the adoption of autonomous vehicles. However, the actual record of autonomous vehicle deaths and injuries so far suggests that there is still work to be done. Furthermore, the available data doesn't yet provide a very complete picture, as autonomous vehicles have only been allowed on public roads in normal driving conditions for a relatively short space of time. Far too many road conditions are as yet untested, and the high-profile fatality involving a Tesla on autopilot has generated some negative sentiment. The evidence base will of course improve as the quantity of trips and the number of miles/kilometers driven rises, and the number of manufacturers of semi- or fully-autonomous vehicles increases. The cars will also become safer with continuous improvement in the underlying autonomous management systems powered by artificial intelligence (AI).

One of the main ways that accidents and casualties will be addressed in self-driving cars is via the AI systems on board. These systems are complex machine learning software applications that draw data from a range of vehicle sensors, learning from experience and an ever-increasing awareness of their surroundings, which are used to update the initial knowledge base they were "trained" with. Not only will the system tap into its own elaborate internal sensor network for information, it will also interact with and learn from other vehicles using vehicle to vehicle (v2v) as well as vehicle to infrastructure (v2i) and vehicle to everything (v2x) communications. The automated car will be a communications hub for many in- and on-vehicle devices (e.g. cameras) and objects (e.g. seats), of which the human occupant is just one. The converging influx of information is assumed to provide an improved safety net, although this is still an unproven hypothesis.

Autonomous vehicles represent an interesting challenge for those involved in vehicle maintenance. Reductions in accident rates would lead to lower demand for recovery and repair services. The upside is that there are an increasing number of upgrade kits becoming available to add varying degrees of autonomy to a conventional vehicle. Fitting these add-ons could become a major revenue stream for repair garages.

Fuel Management

Autonomous vehicles would, by definition, use fossil fuels more efficiently and reliably. They would be programmed for efficiency in a way that would completely unburden the driver from making such decisions. The intention is that the car would always take the most effective routes and waste almost no resources whatsoever. They would also be very well maintained by the vehicle's own "smart" internal systems, so any issues that would cause excessive fuel use could be identified and addressed immediately.

There is an even more promising trend in self-driving vehicles, which is that they are being built with electric or hybrid engines under the hood. Chrysler's new minivan is one example of this shift towards electric vehicle (EV) design. Self-driving cars aren't just changing the way we drive, but offer a huge opportunity to fundamentally transform how mobility is powered.

Traffic Flows

The majority of the Earth's people now live in cities, and that is good news for the autonomous car industry. Cities are "on the grid," and they have an increasingly connected and "intelligent" traffic management set-up—which is what self-driving cars need. At present the required data, connectivity, and infrastructure are only available in big, urban areas. Cities also have the greatest demand for moving people around efficiently. Currently, country highways and back roads aren't equipped for self-driving cars, so they are likely to be an urban phenomenon for the time being.

The other source of demand for these vehicles will come from developing urban areas in the emergent global economies like China and India. Urban growth in these areas are prime for growing "smart," that is, taking advantage of all the technology at their disposal including smartphones and IT for gathering big data about commuter patterns, for example. Building out developing areas with a self-driving mindset would prevent the construction of wasteful infrastructure—like parking lots and multi-lane highways—and allow emergent cities to build smart. That being said, the Indian government has banned autonomous vehicles for the time being, with concerns being their potential impact on driver jobs and public safety.

Taxis

According to *CB Insights* there are over 30 companies working on autonomous vehicles and about half of those are already permitted to use roads in California. Testing these new waters, Uber rolled out and then withdrew a self-driving fleet in California, due to a chorus of controversy and issues. Even more futuristic visions include a self-steering cruise ship, self-flying planes, and self-flying cars. Individual car ownership might be on its way out and soon all passenger cars may essentially become taxis. This in turn leads to the possibility of self-owning assets.

Regulation and Ethics

Regulation is a key uncertainty, but a necessity. Previously the driver's license formed the social compact to enforce norms for those behind the wheel. Now, the responsibility for applying such ethics lies with technology. Do we trust AI in the same way we as trust perfect strangers not to run into us, and to drive us where we need to go? Maybe we can give them as much, or more, trust than a human stranger. Other than the fact that, over time, driving jobs would become rare or extinct, in the near term, input is needed from policy makers, consumers, and industry insiders alike, so that good judgement is exercised to identify and address emerging challenges.

Ultimately, the self-driving vehicle is not about cars or even mobility, but about information. The car is transforming from an impersonal analog machine to a smart and responsive interactive, personalized gadget on wheels—more like a smartphone in the way we think about its utility and how we might pay for it. While there has always been a lot of personal identity wrapped up in automobiles, there was also a clear hierarchy between man and machine; the car was nothing without a driver. This is now changing.

If the current prevailing vision of the future of self-driving cars comes about, we can expect a few key changes. First, an automobile's own awareness and knowledge—about the driver, the places it drives, and other vehicles—will become a valuable, new commercial resource in and of itself. Will getting into a car be like signing into Facebook?

Second, the car industry will no longer be owner-oriented, but sharing-oriented and based on renewable energy instead of fossil fuels. A lot of CO_2 emissions and all kinds of consumer waste will be prevented. Could automobiles also enter a new phase of no ownership, but instead be leased or become a pay-per-use form of mobility?

Third, mobility will live up to its name (mobility, not gridlock) and cities will manage a new source of vulnerability—complete trust in data and technology—in exchange for no traffic. Cities should become more efficient and well managed, and presumably safer, and offer a higher overall quality of life. They will also be more automated and closely surveilled.

The discussion about the future development path, take up, and social impact of self-driving cars will continue for some time to come, and we are at a very early point in the sector's evolution. The journey will continue with many possible routes to the future.

- *Would autonomous vehicle regulation promote or hamper the advancement of this technology?*
- *How would the car as a service business model impact the development of different car designs, branding, and customization?*
- *How might we address the security risks inherent to self-driving cars, like a potential hack?*

A version of this article was originally published in *Disruptive Asia* under the title "Assessing the real impact of autonomous vehicles."

Robo-Retail vs. Humanity at a Price? Two Possible Futures for Retail

By Rohit Talwar, Steve Wells, April Koury, and Alexandra Whittington

What future can we see for humans in retail given the relentless march of the robots?

Much of the current debate on automation focuses on the possible demise of existing jobs and the spread of automation into service and white-collar sectors. Indeed, retail is certainly one industry poised to follow this automation path in pursuit of the next driver of profits. From the advent of the steam engine and mechanization of farming, through to the introduction of personal computing, jobs have always been automated using technology. However, as new technologies have come to market, human ingenuity and the ability to create new products and services have increased the scope for employment and fulfillment. Retail has enjoyed enormous benefits from technology tools, but has the time come when automation poses a threat to jobs? Here we present two possible scenarios for retail 2020-2025: one where automation eliminates most retail jobs and a second which sees the emergence of new paid roles in retail.

Scenario One: Robo-Retail Rules

By 2020, in-store robots walk the aisles to guide customers, help order from another branch, and bring goods to the checkout or your car. Artificial intelligence (AI) personal assistants like Siri and Alexa have become personal shoppers, with perfect knowledge of customers' tastes and preferences. This allows for development of retail algorithms to recommend the perfect item before shoppers even know they want it. The algorithms offer recommendations drawing on databases of consumer preferences (i.e. Amazon recommendations), social media, friends' recent purchases, and analysis of emerging trends—with our AI assistants providing our profiles to help filter and select the appropriate offers.

By 2022, many stores try to retain humans in key service roles for customers who want the personal touch, but most customers prefer to shop online, even if they still browse in-store. Mobile and pop-up digital stores and malls—where customers view products digitally—display selected items as touchable and sniffable holograms personalized to you. Wealthier customers can book a personal visit by an autonomous vehicle, robot, or drone which can then perform the holographic display in the comfort of your own home or garden, giving birth to the next wave of home shopping parties.

In this scenario, TV and retail are fully integrated: Many films and TV shows offer the ability to click on an item in the show, view it in more detail, see how we would look wearing it or how it might look in our home, and then make an instant purchase. In all these formats, shoppers "click to buy" virtual items, which are shipped instantly by autonomous vehicle or drone.

By 2025 the physical stores that continue to attract customers do so with high-tech, in-store experiential services. In-store 3D/4D printing and spray-on manufacture of items to your design are commonplace. Experiences include multi-sensory immersive fashion displays; mirrors showing customers wearing an item of clothing under different lighting, in different colors, and sizes; and robot tailors customizing clothing to our requirements while we wait. The sharing economy is well advanced by now so that, at the point of purchase for many items, we already have a community who will share the ownership and cost of purchase with us.

Scenario Two: Humanity at a Price

By 2020, retailers use AI to determine who typically shops and when, and change displays so that eye-catching items are offered to relevant customers walking through at the time of day they typically visit. This would work particularly well in train stations and airports when you have a sense of which high spending passenger groups are coming through at any given time. In-store robots and drones could continuously change displays, alleviating the repetitive, physically exhausting work of retail jobs. Employees would therefore be more relaxed, thus placing more attention on the customer. Local stores might use AI apps to track the preferences of their customers, make recommendations, and deliver items at the perfect time so that shopping is completely seamless and tailored to specific customer needs. This is the edge by which small brick-and-mortar shops can compete with online retailers and bigger chains.

By 2022, people are willing to pay a premium to access a live purchasing advisor, someone who is an expert in a certain line of retail. This exclusivity leads to super elite retail boutiques. Part of what these shops offer would be a service where shoppers connect with fashion bloggers, Instagram idols, or YouTube artists whose fashion sense they admire. Customer service is anything but free, but well worth the cost to these shoppers. Creativity, self-expression, and individuality are major retail offerings in this future. For example, 3D print stores could help shoppers design an item, then print it while they lunch for them to collect on departure. The value-add of retail work would be the personal touch and connection in creating and selecting personalized products. In this future, services and guides become increasingly important in shopping experiences, especially in destination shopping centers and malls, keeping retail jobs in demand.

By 2025 automation's impact may support retail growth: Products could become so cheap thanks to extremely low-cost, highly-productive robotic labor that the value comes in the form of an evolved "Personal Shopper." Automation and robotics would support the actual purchase and delivery, but a Personal Shopper provides emotional support and companionship on the shopping experience: "That suits you so well…" "Why not cook prawns as a starter if chicken is your main course?" In a future where most people are involved in online schooling and remote working, this Personal Shopper service could meet cravings for personal contact.

Two Retail Futures

There is little debate that robots will take jobs, hence both scenarios assume that the future leads to the automation of current retail roles. Companies, however, must take care to avoid the temptation to plug in technology fixes where human solutions are needed, and this is especially true for retail. The value of a good, authentic conversational style or a sense of humor is something that even today puts certain retail workers at an advantage. Public-facing jobs are a test of social skills, which seem to be safely in the domain of people, not robots, for now.

- *How can we create a harmonic shopping experience that capitalizes on the distinct advantages of both humans and robots?*
- *How will each of these futures respond to high-traffic sale events like Christmas shopping or Black Friday deals?*
- *What kind of retail service might customers prefer ten years from now?*

A version of this article was originally published in *Essential Retail* under the title "Robo-retail vs. humanity at a price?"

Unleashing the True Potential of AI – Building the Exponential Law Firm

By Rohit Talwar

How can the legal sector take advantage of the unprecedented growth opportunity presented by the technological disruption of clients across all sectors?

Artificial intelligence (AI) represents both the biggest opportunity and potentially the greatest threat to the legal profession since its formation. This is part of a bigger global revolution, where society, business, and government are likely to experience more change in the next 20-30 years than in the last 500. This large-scale disruption is being driven by the combinatorial effects of AI and a range of other disruptive technologies whose speed, power, and capability is growing at an exponential rate or faster—and which both enable AI and are fed by it. All of which could literally be hundreds or thousands of times more powerful and impactful within a decade.

The resulting changes are expected to lead to the total transformation of every business sector, the birth of new trillion-dollar industries, and a complete rethink of the law, regulation, legal infrastructures, and the supporting governance systems for literally every activity on the planet.

At present, the sheer scale of the opportunity is lost on all but a few genuinely forward-thinking players across the legal ecosystem. The majority in the sector are either blissfully unaware of what impact AI could have on their market potential, or they are becoming obsessed with the internal applications of AI. In many cases, a natural tendency towards risk aversion is leaving firms paralyzed by fears of declining revenues, commoditization, the depersonalization of the sector, and the loss of professional roles. These fears have in turn driven reluctance to even understand, let alone embrace, the true opportunity presented by AI and other disruptive technologies.

I believe law firms can and should escape from conventional wisdom and look to drive exponential improvements in internal performance and market growth by exploiting the opportunities presented by AI and emerging technologies. Indeed, some in the legal sector are already diving deep to understand what they are and their true commercial potential. However, many are still more worried about the potential negative impacts of AI on the US$650 billion legal services market and are proceeding cautiously as a result. I would argue that the real exponential growth opportunity lies in helping the world respond to the transformative impact of AI on the roughly US$75 trillion global economy.

Driving Internal Transformation

The pace of AI development is stunning, even to those working in the sector. The resounding victory of Google DeepMind's AlphaGo over the world GO champion in March 2016 demonstrated just how far machine learning—the core technology of AI—has evolved. With over 560 million possible moves, the system was not taught to play GO. Instead it was equipped with a sophisticated learning algorithm that allowed it to deduce the rules and possible moves from observing thousands of games. AlphaGo has subsequently been overtaken by a new version, AlphaGo Zero, which trained itself to play Go in three days without human supervision, and then beat AlphaGo by 100 games to zero. This same learning technology can now be used across the various datasets held by law firms. AI has truly transformative potential, with a wide range of legal applications emerging, such as:

- Inferring the likely outcome of a case;
- Determining the best structure for a contract;
- Suggesting how best to approach a new matter; or,
- Making sense of literally billions of data points across the web to spot new and emerging risks and legal threats.

I envisage five broad categories where we will see increasing use of AI within law firms in the next three to five years:

- Automation of legal tasks and processes;
- Decision support and outcome prediction;
- Creation of new product and service offerings;
- Process design and matter management; and,
- Practice management.

In addition, we are likely to see the growing use of AI both by in-house legal teams and in a range of online platforms offering direct services to businesses and individuals. AI will also power developments using blockchain technology (the secure transaction encoding mechanisms that underpin most digital currencies such as Bitcoin), e.g.:

- Smart contracts encoded in software which require no human intervention;
- Distributed autonomous organizations (DAOs) that exist entirely in software with no human employees;
- Decentralized arbitration and mediation networks, which effectively operate as "opt-in" global justice systems for commercial transactions, and which sit outside the existing national and global mechanisms;
- Algocracy or Algorithmic Democracy, i.e. creating global codes of legal transacting by codifying and automating legal documents, including contracts, permits, organizational documents, and consents; and,
- Rewriting and embedding the law in software, e.g. automatic fines, drawing evidence from the Internet of things (IoT), standardized open source legal documents, and automated judgments.

How Might AI Evolve Within the Sector?

Here is a plausible timeline of AI developments in the legal sector over the next five years—while some may proceed with even greater caution, a number may reach these milestones far faster.

The Next 18 Months
- Growth of law firms establishing internal technology innovation labs, creating seed funds to invest in legal technology start-ups, and running joint experiments with technology providers and clients;
- A number of firms and in-house teams will run AI trials and develop applications that create smarter internal processes;
- A range of trials and applications of AI for lawyer decision support;
- Launch of the first client facing AI applications and new AI-enabled products and services;
- Growth of FinTech—the rising pressure from financial services to embrace AI/blockchain technology—with legal cost reduction a key driver; and,
- Emergence of blockchain smart contracts and DAO's.

The Next Three Years
- Clear evidence of lawyer replacement by smart technologies;
- Widespread and accelerating deployment of AI on core law firm processes;
- Meaningful penetration of AI into in-house legal;
- First truly AI-centric law firms;
- Significant range of AI-based solutions offered direct to consumers and SMEs/technology businesses; and,
- Widespread adoption of blockchain smart contracts in newer firms/rise of DAOs in both the private and public sectors.

The Next Five Years
- Applications starting to emerge that display near-human levels of intelligence (artificial general intelligence) in certain

domains;
- First examples of true Algocracy—countries moving to digitizing/automating/embedding the law;
- Blockchain/smart contracts/DAOs in widespread use in financial services and other sectors;
- 20-50% of "routine" legal work by sector fully automated by clients with no law firm involvement;
- New technology-centric legal sector entrants from the last five years competing head on with Big Law; and,
- AI in widespread use across law firms and frequently mandated by clients.

Going for the Bigger Prize

Whilst AI can clearly be disruptive within law firms, the real AI transformation opportunity lies in the broader marketplace. Indeed, by focusing almost exclusively on the internal impact on the roughly US$650 billion legal services market, the sector is missing the point. I believe that AI—combined with the other disruptive technologies mentioned—could redefine every existing business sector and drive the creation of new ones, leading to dramatic growth of the global economy to US$120 trillion or more in the next decade.

AI and the technologies it enables such as robotics, blockchain, MedTech, EdTech, and FinTech will drive the reinvention of existing sectors from media, healthcare, education, and transport to retail, construction, and financial services. AI is already enabling the next wave of trillion-dollar sectors and developments such as autonomous vehicles, DAOs, synthetic biology, smart materials, intelligent cities, blockchain data networks, and smart contracts. AI is also driving interest in new economic paradigms, new notions of money, and new legal models such as Algocracy.

All these developments will require the interpretation, reframing, and redrafting of legal frameworks. They will also drive the creation of updated legal concepts and dispute resolution mechanisms to encompass new political, economic, social, and business paradigms. So, while AI will undoubtedly have a transformative impact on how law firms work internally, the true exponential growth opportunity lies in helping governments, businesses, and civil society to understand, regulate for, and adjust to the coming waves of AI-enabled disruption.

Here are a few examples of those new legal sector opportunities we envisage emerging as sectors are transformed by successive waves of technology:

- Establishing the governing principles and regulations around the use and insurance of self-driving vehicles;
- Rollback, recovery, contract review, and dispute arbitration for fully automated, blockchain-based financial transaction systems;
- Governance and "right of redress" protocols where AI systems are replacing human decision makers in areas as diverse as healthcare, social security, and legal dispute resolution;
- Usage control and privacy protection within the AI systems that will manage and interpret the massive data flows arising from the Internet of Things;
- Creating regulatory frameworks to govern the conduct of and dispute resolution for DAOs; and,
- Determining governance and monitoring frameworks for science research, which is designed and conducted entirely by AI systems, e.g. the creation of new life forms.

Over the next five to ten years, we will see these and many more opportunities arise as existing sectors are transformed and new ones emerge. AI and related technologies will enable the creation of entirely new markets, commercial concepts, business models, and delivery mechanisms, ideas that we couldn't even begin to imagine or describe today. For forward thinking law firms, these developments offer the potential to drive exponential growth in revenues—if we give ourselves permission to invest the time understanding these brave new world technologies and their transformative potential. Whether firms seize the opportunity or become paralyzed by fear and indecision will ultimately be a matter of choice and a function of our willingness to step into the unknown and start learning.

- *How can the legal sector overcome a traditional culture of caution to embrace the opportunities presented by cutting edge advances on the horizon?*

- *What critical changes in organizational mindset would contribute most to enabling future waves of innovation in legal?*

- *How could small and medium law firms take advantage of the "paralyzing" effect AI may have on bigger firms?*

A version of this article was originally published in *Barrister Magazine.*

A Day in the Life of a Legal Project Manager: June 1st, 2020

By Rohit Talwar and Alexandra Whittington

How will "business as usual" be conducted in tomorrow's law firm after the Fourth Industrial Revolution?

Recently we have seen exponential growth in the discussion of, and experimentation with, the use of artificial intelligence (AI) in legal, with an increasing focus on the project management domain.

Given that such applications have already been discussed and assessed quite widely elsewhere, we decided to wind the clock forward to explore how the potential applications of AI in legal project management could evolve over the next three to five years. To this end, presented below is a scenario of what might be possible by 2020 in the more advanced adopters of AI in legal.

Janet Goes to Work: Monday June 1st, 2020

9:00 am Monday June 1st, 2020, Janet reports to work as a legal project manager at the shared office building where her law firm leases co-working space. The start time to her day is the only traditional thing about her job.

Janet works for NFW, a top 20 global law firm, which relocated in 2019 from a plush city center office building to a cluster of practical and economical co-working cooperatives in key cities around the world. The legal team shares conference rooms and some support staff with the other tenants, which include technology start-ups, graphic designers, and consulting firms. The working space is diverse and a bit chaotic, but always occupied. When not being used as office space, the building is used for pop-up adult education courses, retail shops, and civic meetings. This saves NFW money and helps build a presence in the community, giving a local feel to their global firm.

NFW's previous location was a beautiful old building that used only fossil fuel energy, and was poorly retrofitted with the efficiency boosting detectors, beacons, and transmitters that today's smart offices rely on. Plus, it was very expensive real estate. The new network of shared offices is cheaper, more ecologically sound, and much more high-tech. Furthermore, the reduced overheads allow the firm to spend more on IT and HR, two areas where the legal industry is finally starting to see significant returns on investment.

The AI-Enabled Project Manager

NFW was one of the first of the global law firms to pioneer a new client service model where an AI-enabled project manager is assigned to orchestrate the conduct of a matter from the outset. The legal sector has seen an increasing technology component in many projects and the growing use of non-legal staff including business consultants, researchers, and accountants. Hence, most law firms eventually succumbed and decided to put in place legal project managers to ensure the effective integration and co-ordination of all other elements involved to deliver the desired outcomes to the client.

While some lawyers objected to what they felt was an undermining of their roles, others appreciated the time it freed up for them to focus on providing sound business-orientated legal advice and keeping their own expertise up to date. A key by-product of this team approach coupled with the use of AI billing tools has been a massive reduction in billing disputes, write-offs, and payment delays, issues which many lawyers had traditionally found uncomfortable raising with clients.

The Personal Digital Assistant: Lawrence

The workday begins with a chat with her personal digital legal assistant, Lawrence, an AI helper who has been with Janet for a year now. Although Janet has a very personal relationship with Lawrence, he is in fact a firm-wide legal management environment that effectively supports all aspects of legal project management and provides personal assistant services to professional staff across the firm.

Lawrence was programmed to respond to moods and promote the mental and emotional well-being of its human companion. Today, Lawrence notices from Janet's biometric data feeds that she is tired; she worked all weekend from her home-office. Lawrence communicates to the smart coffee machine to make Janet's cup extra strong so that she can get started on her busy day. He switches on some ambient music which relaxes her. Janet doesn't even realize that Lawrence has embedded some productivity enhancing tracks alongside the soft music that welcomes her. The sounds were designed just for Janet, based on her biometric feeds and Lawrence's knowledge of her musical preferences, gained from talking to the AI on her phone and monitoring her social media profiles.

HR ensures that worker productivity at the firm is kept at a maximum by using personalized approaches to stress-reduction and efficiency. A biological and genetic profile of each employee is created for the purpose of customizing their environment to enhance each individual worker's potential. Janet is quickly revitalized and together she and Lawrence begin to review the day's activities.

The Daily Briefing

Lawrence uses hologram displays to show Janet the daily briefing. The first thing on the agenda is to review the dossiers on the clients involved in a potentially big M&A case the firm is bidding on. Full profiles of the companies and the key executives involved in the merger begin appearing in a 3D video Lawrence has compiled with an amalgamation of data gleaned from the internet and their social media profiles.

The presentation gives her a better understanding of the client's history, motivations, and the context of the project. Above all, it provides the information necessary for the team to communicate effectively with these clients about the details of the merger and NFW's understanding of the subtleties of the transaction. This also allows Janet and the lawyers she works with to provide a special finesse to the account management, billing, and scheduling part of each working relationship.

Preparing for a Virtual Meeting

To create the video, Lawrence trawled the internet, as well as several large databases, to pull in relevant, up-to-the-minute transaction related details for the virtual meeting scheduled for 10 am. The information is presented in a way that Janet is most comfortable with: visual and image-based. Lawrence confirms that the lead lawyer, Sarah, is happy with the content, and that she is ready to join Janet in this virtual call with the clients.

Sarah will offer the customized detailed legal service package Lawrence has prepared to the exact specifications of the various contributing team members—with oversight from Janet. It took a while to get the teams working in this highly collaborative AI-enabled manner, but the model is working well now. The team building, co-ordination, and conflict resolution skills of the project manager are recognized as the critical differentiator between the best performing projects and the rest. With what Janet now knows about the client—their likes, dislikes, habits, and history as analyzed by her AI assistant—she realizes they are possibly going to ask for alternative service options beyond the bid Lawrence has created.

Considering Alternate Delivery Options

Lawrence can provide a set of delivery options with associated pricing, ranging from highly automated execution through to heavy personal involvement from the lawyers and other key members of the team. The more human involvement, the more expensive the job, but this has become a hallmark of the legal industry, and Janet knows that clients appreciate having this range of choices to select from.

Often, particularly with more complex matters and new developments such as the introduction of autonomous vehicles and human enhancement centers, the clients involved are willing to spend more to get the input and oversight of human experts. There are, however, an increasing number of situations where clients accept that, for the matter in hand, a "robolawyer" will be just as good—and much more cost-effective—than a person. The firm is not bashful about this reality. Law firm automation is not just happening in the management and accounting functions; it is helping to redefine the entire firm and most other white-collar industries.

Lawrence Multi-Tasking
Lawrence performs several jobs, but his most important contribution is the ability to analyze ever larger data sets to extract usable information for bids and proposals, spot interesting patterns, correlations, and anomalies, and help apply that knowledge to proposal development, project planning, and workflow management. One of the main benefits of Lawrence's software is the ability to predict case outcomes. Form the early 2010s onwards, a range of innovative software tools such as Lex Machina started to emerge, predicting the outcome of court cases based on previous results.

Lawrence's Proprietary Enhancement
NFW believes there is still competitive advantage to be gained in this arena and has developed a proprietary algorithm within Lawrence which takes all the factors of a legal matter into account. Lawrence compares the case information to previous cases in public databases, and then determines the probability, costs, and likely financial impacts of a range of possible outcomes.

The ability to predict outcomes has technically lost the firm revenue, as clients won't pursue a case if Lawrence believes the results won't be in their favor. The loss of litigation revenue is not a dramatic as some NFW lawyers had first feared, as the firm is able to charge a premium for the advice and effective management of early settlements following analysis by Lawrence. Moreover, the resulting reduction in legal costs to clients has won the loyalty of many important clients and has shown the firm to be a source of solid, evidence-based advice.

Lawrence also predicts the time and costs involved in each case down to the minute and penny, with its accuracy becoming ever higher in light of learning from previous case data; hence, clients that choose to take a case to court can do so confident in the likely outcome and associated costs. NFW's AI outcome prediction strategy has earned it an excellent reputation for putting client needs first, having never lost a case since its implementation. This implicit guarantee of customer satisfaction has helped drive exponential improvement in the rates of revenue growth, client attrition, and new client acquisition.

Skills of AI-Enabled Legal Project Managers

After lunch Janet checks on the progress of new applicants to work with her in a (human) junior project manager role. The firm uses AI enabled gamification based on role playing real life client scenarios to identify and recruit job candidates, a trend that is really starting to take root in the sector. The idea is to identify those who have the technical knowledge, social skills, and emotional intelligence to perform effectively in dynamic multi-disciplinary client facing teams. The firm's website and social media pages include a link to the game, and high scorers are invited to submit CVs when there are new job openings.

Instead of having a huge file of résumés to read through, Janet checks the scores and team behaviors of the latest batch of applicants. She sees that one candidate, a graduate of an online university, has some very good point scores on the core technical and social interaction requirements, but is also doing well on the strategy and critical thinking criteria, which the gamers probably don't even realize they are being tested on. Janet remembers a day when her children's school experienced an unexpected closure and she had to bring her 10-year-old son to work with her. She let him play the recruitment game all afternoon and he had no idea that it was anything different from the video games he played at home—and Lawrence said his scores suggested he'd make a great lawyer!

Working with Big Brother

Before the day's end, there would be a big meeting related to the new hire. There would be several departments represented there, including IT, since the candidate needed to have some fairly strong coding experience. The person would be working alongside Janet and Lawrence to train a new piece of AI software, one which, for now, they jokingly call "Big Brother."

Essentially a surveillance technology, the new AI takes the form of a wearable device meant for lawyers. It would be placed on the person's body, having the appearance of a badge or piece of jewelry, but it would be made up of cameras, sensors, and recording devices to monitor the entire workday's activity. One result of all this will be to improve and simplify the billing process. The device can even pick up on the lawyer's brain patterns to identify when he or she was thinking about a client, to capture all billable moments.

With Big Brother, the firm is hoping to pioneer a "to-the-second" billing structure, which would allow profits to grow while ensuring the highest possible accuracy in billing. Given the software can also recognize the difference between deep thought, reflection, analysis, and more routine review and drafting tasks, this allows for truly differential pricing for different tasks performed by the same person. This would also allow lawyers to focus more on the core aspects of their job, and make roles like Janet's much easier. She and her staff (with their AI helpers, of course) should now be able to analyze and monitor the device output in real-time and prepare detailed financial reports at the request of the lawyers, the finance department, or the client—this is where the coding skills come in.

Providing Client Insight

Another "as-a-service" niche the firm is hoping to fill is that of litigation data analysis, providing clients with detailed insights into the time and resources spent on legal services both by their law firms and their own internal legal departments. Hence, the new hybrid role would work with IT, HR, and legal project management—so there would be a lot of cross-over involved, something Janet was seeing increasingly with the new project team approach. The sensitive nature of the data being handled by Big Brother meant HR needed to be involved to monitor both the human analyst's adherence to privacy rules and the evolving behavior of the system itself, to make sure it didn't start to cross ethical boundaries as it adapted and evolved.

As Janet was leaving the office she saw that the conference room where they held their meeting today was being set up for a learn-to-code class. She thought of possibly taking the course herself, coding being something she never learned in her youth, when it was really cutting-edge. Maybe she could learn to reprogram Lawrence to order her a lower strength morning coffee and turn down the welcome music.

- *How might the role IT of departments in law firms need to evolve to ensure it can drive deep innovation and stay relevant to the needs of the business?*
- *In an increasingly automated environment, what would be the main motivations for human employees to go to work?*
- *How would we control the occurrence and monitoring of politically incorrect thoughts if Big Brother is always on?*

A version of this article was originally published in *Legal Project Management.*

Most Exponential Law Firms 2025

By Rohit Talwar and Alexandra Whittington

What new law firm business models might emerge as a result of using exponential technologies?

Exponential Fever

The business world is currently gripped by exponential fever. The concept came to prominence with Moore's law—the doubling every 18-24 months of the amount of computer power available for $1,000. The phenomenon has since been replicated in many fields of science and technology. We now see the speed, functionality, and performance of a range of technologies growing at an exponential rate. Applications encompass everything from data storage capacity and video download speed, to the time taken to map a genome and the cost of producing a laboratory grown hamburger.

New Pretenders

A wave of new economy businesses has now brought exponential thinking to bear in transforming assumptions about how an industry works. For example, Airbnb handles roughly 90 times more bedroom listings per employee than the average hotel group, while Tangerine Bank can service seven times more customers than a typical competitor. In automotive, by adopting 3D printing, Local Motors can develop a new car model 1,000 times cheaper than traditional manufacturers, with each car coming "off the line" 5 to 22 times faster. In response, businesses in literally every sector are pursuing exponential improvement in everything from new product development and order fulfillment, through to professional productivity and the rate of revenue growth.

Stepping Up

For law firms, the transformation of other sectors and their accompanying legal frameworks creates a massive growth opportunity, coupled with the potential to bring a similar approach to rethinking the way law firms operate. While some might be hesitant about applying these disruptive technologies internally, there is a clear opportunity to be captured from helping clients respond to these developments and from the creation of the industries of the future. To help bring to life the possibilities within legal, we highlight seven scenarios that illustrate how exponential change could transform law firms over the next 5 to 10 years.

Rise of the "Exponential Circle"

Our continuing program of research on the future of law firms suggests that we will see exponential growth for those firms who can both master the legal implications of these technologies for their clients and become adept at their application within the firm. By 2025, we could indeed have witnessed the emergence of an "Exponential Circle" of law firms who have reached escape velocity and left the rest behind.

Dancing with the Disruptors

This accelerated growth opportunity is being driven by the combinatorial effects of artificial intelligence (AI), and a range of other disruptive technologies, whose speed, power, and capability are increasing at an exponential rate or faster. The resulting changes will lead to the total transformation of every business sector, the birth of new trillion-dollar industries, and a complete rethink of the law, regulation, legal infrastructures, and the supporting governance systems for every activity on the planet.

Tools of Future Exploration

As futurists, one of our core tools for making sense of a range of emerging trends, forces, ideas, and developments is to combine them into scenarios of alternate possible futures; stories are one of the key ways in which we share our ideas. We find these far more powerful than predictions, as they allow organizations to prepare for a range of plausible futures rather than relying on more restrictive predictive perspectives and forecasts. The scenarios that follow are built upon factual evidence gained through our research on current and emerging developments, and a resulting set of well-supported assumptions about how developments might play out. These are bound together with some creative conjecture to create storylines that are designed to provoke thought and debate and impart the difference between today and possible tomorrows.

Category Winners

Below we envision what the winners would look like if we were to travel forward in time to meet the recipients of seven of the global awards for the Most Exponential Law Firms of 2025.

Category 1: Applications that Display Near-Human Levels of Intelligence—or Artificial General Intelligence (AGI)—in Certain Domains

Winner: Hothouse Lawyers, a law firm that has formally eliminated entry-level positions. Instead they are filled by an AGI or AI so that highly-paid human lawyers focus their efforts on the more skilled tasks that require their experience, expertise, and intuition. The AI-based legal support systems learn, adapt, and evolve with the needs of the professionals they support. They even conduct a significant amount of client interaction—often with an AI-based intelligent assistant at the other end. This combination of smart, market-focused lawyers underpinned by wide-ranging AI has enabled industry leading exponential improvement in both operational performance and profit growth.

Hothouse Lawyers is named after its reputation for tender culti-vation of the few attorneys it employs: Lawyers are treated like rare orchids in a highly inhospitable climate. The legal hiring freezes of the early 2020s resulted in the average age of an attorney rising to 60, exacerbated by the fact that retirement has been eliminated across most professions. Job security has also gone exponential, and employ-ment, for those who can find it, is for life. Only senior positions exist in the firm, and the lawyers who fill them are protected from anything but the most rarefied legal work. All the research assistants have been outsourced or automated, but there are new service jobs created for human personal assistants to these celebrity-like lawyers. The assistants earn low wages although their bosses' seven-figure salaries seem to increase exponentially, as do the life expectancies of these highly-compensated figureheads.

Hothouse relies on other firms to do the initial training of lawyers, with several law schools also stepping into this space. Hothouse and other similar firms now pay a hiring or "transfer" fee to the firms and law schools from which they recruit more experienced lawyers.

Category 2: Implementation of True Algorithmic Democracy (Algocracy) - Supporting the Move to Digitizing, Automating, and Embedding the Law

Winner: Jónsdóttir & Jónsson, the most innovative law firm in Iceland during the early post-Algocracy period and a pioneer in the design and deployment of Algocracy solutions globally.

Following a series of failed government coalitions since early 2017 and the Panama Papers II leak in 2019, Iceland's citizens decided to overthrow the current government, with the hope of creating a more transparent, democratic, and simpler governance model. In a process stewarded by the Pirate Party, Iceland's entire political, legal, and financial governance system was converted into an Algocracy, or law by algorithm. Drawing on examples from pioneers in Algocracy such as Singapore and the United Arab Emirates, Icelanders decided that they could no longer trust their human overlords and decided to take their chances with code instead. The combination of a wealthy, egalitarian, and educated population coupled with a history of radical political activism made Iceland a perfect fit for the next step towards a form of technological singularity.

Iceland proved to be the perfect testing ground for Algocracy and the automation of legal and political decision making. A culture of open-mindedness permitted public trust in AI to grow, while the revolutionary political context ensured that high levels of civic oversight of technology were embedded in the system. The law is embedded at every level; our cars fine us if we speed, and automated courts now draw on data from sensors in objects at the crime scene connected via the Internet of things (IoT). The law firm of Jónsdóttir & Jónsson is recognized for pioneering the concepts of Algocracy at the nation scale, leading the design and implementation of the solutions and for its innovation in dealing with Iceland's civil, corporate, criminal, and tax law in the transition period.

In addition to helping the nation avoid complete anarchy during the first two years of Algocracy, the firm has effectively become the "global go-to" advisory partner on all aspects of algorithmic law. Jónsdóttir & Jónsson has shown the importance of adding software developers, political scientists, and ethicists to legal teams to design effective systems and back-up provision for nations where human intelligence is ceding to the wisdom of machines.

Since its pioneering work in the field with an Algocracy team of four among a practice of 20 lawyers in its sole office in Reykjavik in 2017, the firm has grown to over 800 staff working on Algocracy issues in 60 cities and 40 countries around the world. The pioneering risk and reward sharing business model has also put Jónsdóttir & Jónsson in the top five globally in terms of profit per partner.

Category 3: Blockchain/Smart Contracts/Distributed Autonomous Organizations (DAOs)
Winner: Ether Law, a Boston based pioneer in distributed law, has become a global leader in helping firms, industry sectors, regulators,

governments, and law enforcement agencies adapt to a blockchain world. The use of blockchain-like mutual distributed ledger systems first came to prominence with the rise of Bitcoin, the digital currency that sits outside the regulation of governments and central banks. The transactions are encoded in a highly secure manner and recorded in multiple electronic ledgers distributed across global networks.

Ether Law recognized the opportunity to use such technology in domains as diverse as asset provenance and real estate transactions, through to verification of academic qualifications and the tracking and tracing of international criminals. While other much larger firms adopted a "wait and see" attitude, Ether Law took a proactive stance in encouraging clients to explore the use of blockchain solutions. The firm focused on helping to define the underlying legal and contractual infrastructure, and developing the necessary rollback, recovery, and dispute resolution mechanisms. Ether Law pioneered the development of "off the shelf" solutions that enable counter parties to enter into fully automated contracts. They were also a leader in the creation of truly "smart" contracts where the systems can deal with contract variations and anomalies, and negotiate agreed outcomes—without human involvement in over 90% of cases.

A key area in which Ether Law took a lead was in helping to take DAOs into the mainstream and securing their legal status. These businesses exist entirely in software and typically have no employees. The firm has helped new entrants, existing businesses, investors, and governments create DAOs and the mechanisms to regulate them. The firm has grown from 200 professionals and 44 partners in four US offices in 2017, to over 1,000 professionals in 90 countries globally, with over 600 specializing in blockchain related activities.

Category 4: Direct Service Innovation
Winner: ALF, the "Anti-Law Firm," a corporate venturing initiative from one of the large law firms, aimed at pioneering a radically different legal service model. ALF employs a large IT innovation team creating fully automated smart AI and blockchain-based applications running on the internet. These are aimed at consumers, start-ups, and

small to medium sized firms. ALF has fewer than ten senior lawyers acting in an advisory role to an army of chatbots. A key feature is that all its profits are reinvested in service developments, technology tools, and innovative applications—many of which have been adopted by its parent or licensed for use by other law firms.

The Anti-Law Firm is a response to a grassroots movement of coders, computer scientists, and attorneys who decided to put the power of the law back into the hands of the people. Inspired by the early success of DoNotPay, the ALF chatbots have supported millions of people who were previously prevented from remedying legal wrongs because of the high cost of legal representation. It all started with the protests in the late 2010s, which came to be known as Occupy Law.

Occupy Law was at first a US/UK student-debt awareness movement, but later a driving force for a civic renaissance about the right to legal representation. By 2020, citizens were using chatbots to fight their way out of disproportionate student loan debts, tackling unfair housing regulations, and taking on pension and retirement systems rigged against the consumer's best interests. What started as an easy way to protest a parking ticket had turned into a social and criminal justice revolution, which then morphed into the emergence of firms like ALF. Today, the chatbots are all open source, and there are a variety of options to deal with a range of laws and clientele. Because the service is so decentralized and automated, the loosely-organized outfit does not actually consider itself a law firm; nevertheless, the sheer volume of cases it handles mean it is recognized as a leading innovator in exponential legal practices with a focus on DIY law.

Category 5: New Entrants

Winner: Fähig, the law app for the sharing gig economy, is often described as the Uber of legal services. Fähig offers a preventative or preemptive legal service and legal protection by subscription and on-demand. Fähig addresses two key opportunities: firstly the growth in citizens wanting protection of their rights and privacy, and secondly lawyers wanting to offer services globally.

No lawyers, no offices, no actual conference room. If this doesn't sound like the typical law firm, that's because it's not. Fähig (German for "capable, able, competent, proficient") is the legal AI start-up that finally enabled even the smallest of law practices to offer a truly global service via the internet. Lawyers can work cross-jurisdiction thanks to the regulatory acrobatics Fähig is willing to perform in highlighting the relevant country specific laws, precedents, and cases for any matter.

Fähig earns revenues from charging a small subscriber fee for lawyers and clients and taking a small commission for connecting lawyers to clients worldwide. Clients pay a super-low monthly fee for legal service on retainer, which is increasingly a necessity in a surveillance society. In most cases this can be bundled into the customer's bank charges, mobile phone bills, or accessed via a single keystroke on a mobile phone app. Essentially, tap an icon and a lawyer is at your service.

The opportunity was born out of the rise of the "always on always monitored" surveillance society. Increasing digitization of our lives, rising levels of digital policing in many big cities, as well as the explosion of surveillance technologies in the burgeoning smart cities have made it far more common for citizens to be accused of crimes, experience cyber-crime, or suffer identity theft. The proliferation of IoT-enabled devices, city-wide sensor networks, and drone surveillance in the skies means that nothing goes unnoticed or unrecorded. The data is captured in the cloud, shared, and analyzed by ever-smarter technologies.

The "precog" science fiction of the film *Minority Report* has become a reality. Data collection from our mobile devices and the internet has become so efficient that predictive marketing has given way to predictive policing. This has created a high demand for legal advice on how to defend yourself when predictively accused of a crime you have never contemplated or have yet to commit.

Fähig also has a strong customer base of civilians worried that the data they share, their internet searches, and other digital footprints might end up being misused or used against them. So, there is a growing demand for on-demand legal services related to "data and identity theft and misuse protection," and this is the booming specialist market Fähig has been able to serve.

The firm has seen the number of global customers rise from 20,000 in 2018, to over 50 million worldwide by 2025, with revenues topping US$1.5 billion. The firm is owned by a combination of the citizens and lawyers who use it, governments, and technology companies. For law firms, Fähig has also become a training ground for new lawyers as they can be seconded to work within its core team—developing the global jurisdiction analysis systems at the heart of the firm. Many larger firms have also licensed the technology for use with their own clients.

Category 6: Most Disruptive AI Innovation
Winner: My AIAttorneys "In-House" legal service that operates strictly through AI-analyzed surveillance of clients. All research is conducted via monitoring/eavesdropping on the client's computer systems, transaction flows, personal digital assistants, social media activity, emails, and data collected from spy drones, IoT-connected sensors, microphones, and speakers. Today's time-poor legal clients prefer to not have to spend time discussing the details with their attorneys, so instead they give permissions for AIs to observe, collect data, analyze, and predict the information needed for legal representation. The service is particularly popular with the new wave of technology-centric start-ups with big ambitions but very small headcounts—where literally no one has the time or inclination to talk to their lawyers—however important the matter is.

Attorney-client contracts with My AIAttorneys involve permissions to monitor the client, their business, and their key staff at all times, both online and in person. The relationships are two-way; the client's own AI personal assistants, digital twins, drones, or other personal "things" hooked up to the IoT will communicate all the necessary information, knowledge, and experiences, as well as keep tabs on their case and attorney. The service continues to evolve with the firm now able to predict and pre-empt emerging risks in addition to handling existing cases.

Still in its infancy, this service is light years ahead of the simplistic "robolawyers" of the mid-2010s. My AIAttorneys received the award for their innovative "In-House" product, a comprehensive analytics program that collects data on the client 24/7 by use of wearables, implantables, and biometrics in and around their work and home. My AIAttorneys is another example of the growing array of legal firm and technology company hybrids. The combined use of big data, IoT, drones, AI, and next generation real-time e-discovery gives this company an edge unmatched by the rest.

Since launch in 2019, the firm has grown from around 120 individual customers and 15 corporate clients, to over 12,000 individual and 800 business clients ranging from start-ups to now global multi-billion-dollar corporations. Revenues topped US$100 million in 2025.

Category 7: A Very Human Law Firm

Winner: Mann, Mann, and McMann, a British boutique law firm that caters to specialized clientele seeking human lawyers, which are considered a luxury item.

Mann, Mann, and McMann achieves exponential profit growth with a "less is more" attitude to legal services. With just five lawyers on staff and minimal automation outside of routine office processes, this ultra-premium fee firm occupies a spacious and plush office space in London's Mayfair. Client correspondence is handled face to face, over the telephone, and via courier delivered documents. Only in the most extreme of circumstances and for international clients is email used. Text messaging and social media contact with clients is strictly forbidden. In many respects, the firm looks more like the private office of a wealthy family, with no client issue considered out of bounds for the right fee. From helping you sell your company and drawing up prenuptial contracts, through to meeting with your child's boarding school headmaster or commissioning, insuring, and storing bespoke jewelry for you, Mann, Mann, and McMann can deliver.

Each lawyer is supported by six to ten staff who undertake rigorous legal research, conduct forensic-level due diligence of their client's activities and lifestyles, and cater to every need and whim of these rock star lawyers and the clients they serve. The firm is the epitome of elite—with offices replete with rare art, expensive furniture, and five-star catering, these lawyers' reputations for being "divas" is well known. This old-school firm stands out for its adherence to a non-cyborg, AI, or chatbot lawyer tradition.

All five partners are non-enhanced humans and rely solely on their own experience, expertise, intuition, and track record, which are exquisite, exemplary, and costly. The firm has a minimum three-year prepaid retainer with its clients, and charges roughly three times the closest competing firms' fees. Many competitors' can charge lower prices thanks to their investment in intelligent technologies implemented to augment or replace the work of human lawyers.

Mann, Mann, and McMann's clients are typically royalty, multi-millionaires, billionaires, heads of state, leading politicians, sports personalities, and rock stars. These clients value privacy and place a premium on the fact that their affairs are handled by trusted individuals with only the barest minimum of information stored and processed on computers. With the aim of doubling fee rates every three years and participating in the financial success of clients' business ventures and investments, this highly secretive firm has grown average revenues to a reported £7 million per partner. Rumors suggest that unsolicited success payments from clients of £1 million or more are not uncommon.

Seizing the Opportunity

Through these examples, we have tried to highlight a range of ways in which law firms can take advantage of the exponential growth opportunity arising from disruptive technological change. Hopefully we have demonstrated that there are many routes via which technologies such as AI will create new market opportunities, drive change in internal operations, and lead to the emergence of radically new legal service models and opportunities. We could also see the emergence of firms that emphasize the human factor while those around them are eliminating their differentiating features through automation. The thing that all these examples have in common is the potential to drive exponential improvements in performance and the rate of revenue and profit growth. We feel this is an opportunity worth exploring.

- *What might be the key forms of competitive advantage that will help law firms to standout over the next decade?*
- *How might the drive for exponential growth in the legal industry improve customer satisfaction?*
- *How will law firms strive to create synergy between humans and robot employees?*

A version of this article was originally published in *Society for Computers and Law.*

Artificial Intelligence and the Growth Opportunity for Accounting Firms

By Rohit Talwar and Steve Wells

How can accountancy firms tap into the new service possibilities emerging from an AI-enabled economy?

Artificial intelligence (AI) is rising to the top of the business agenda. Literally every day we see ever-more breathtaking announcements of its capabilities from researchers and technology vendors. We also see increasingly stark warnings of its potential to automate knowledge, expertise, and advice-based sectors such as accountancy and thus render millions of professionals unemployed in its wake.

Within the sector, many firms are already deep into their exploration of the potential uses of AI inside their firms and advising clients on potential AI opportunities and impacts. However, hesitancy still dominates management thinking, with innovation being held back by fears about the potential for AI to automate, and eventually commoditize, large parts of a US$450 billion global sector.

We believe these concerns are missing the bigger picture opportunity—namely that every sector in the US$75 trillion global economy will be transformed by the combined effects of AI and a range of other technologies in the fields of computing, communications, genetics, and materials sciences. The speed, power, scope, and capability of these disruptive change agents are growing at an exponential rate or faster. These technologies individually and in combination with each other will enable solutions many times more powerful than anything we can imagine today.

This combination of exponential technology and the new ideas they enable will drive renewal of every industry, and enable the emergence of trillion-dollar sectors. They will also lead to a complete rethinking of business models, accountancy standards, risk assessment approaches, financial reporting practices, legal and regulatory frameworks, and the supporting governance systems for every aspect of our world. Indeed, over the next decade, the global economy could reach US$120 trillion with over 50% coming from emerging sectors and businesses and those that don't even exist today.

Servicing this new world offers the potential for exponential growth and a fundamental rethinking of strategy and execution in accounting firms. The scale of this opportunity seems lost on or ignored by all but the most genuinely forward-thinking players in the sector. The majority are either unaware of AI's potential impact or focused on relatively narrow internal applications of AI. Decision making is clouded by fears of commoditizing premium revenue streams, losing out to technology providers, depersonalization, and the loss of professional roles. These fears have in turn driven reluctance to understand and embrace the real opportunities that could emerge as AI and its disruptive relations facilitate the reinvention of our world.

There are clearly benefits to be gained from automating internal functions and building real-time accounting and audit analytics into clients' transactional systems. The technologies should also help provide rigorous and comprehensive decision support to professionals in key areas of legislative complexity, and automate the analysis of client financials. However, the potential gains are almost trivial compared to the opportunities that arise from supporting the emergence of the AI-enabled new economy.

Winning in the Next Economy

From healthcare to financial services and shipping, the rise of AI will enable the total transformation of every sector of the economy. Industry renewal and the emergence of new trillion-dollar sectors will be fueled by developments such as synthetic fuels, self-repairing construction materials, intelligent cities, autonomous vehicles, 3D printed buildings, superfast Hyperloop rail transit systems, blockchain data networks, smart contracts, and employee free distributed autonomous organizations. Combined with and powered by AI, the next wave of technologies is driving the potential for new economic paradigms, global digital currencies, and new notions of money and tradeable assets.

This scale of change will in turn drive the re-interpretation, reframing, and redrafting of accountancy standards and practices, audit procedures, risk management, valuation techniques, and reporting frameworks Disruption will also lead to the creation of new accounting and legal concepts and financial dispute resolution mechanisms to encompass new political, economic, social, and business paradigms. So, AI will undoubtedly have a big impact on the internal functioning of accounting firms. However, the true exponential growth opportunity lies in helping governments, businesses, and civil society to understand, account for, adjust to, and manage the risks of the coming waves of AI-enabled disruption.

Here are a few examples of these new accounting sector opportunities that are emerging:

- The emergence of autonomous self-driving vehicles opens up the potential for self-owning assets including buildings and public infrastructure—what new accounting practices would be required to govern, audit, and assess the viability of this new asset class?
- New business models such as per second pricing for insurance will require new approaches to accounting, risk, and viability assessment;
- How will we account for transactions conducted in digital currencies and via blockchains where the source of the

funds and information is not known and traditional money laundering rules may be impossible to administer?

- What are the accounting procedures required for rollback, recovery, contract review, and dispute arbitration for fully automated, blockchain-based financial transaction systems?
- How should we account for and address the taxation implications of firms that are using AI systems to move their financial assets around the world on a continuous basis in real time to attract the best second-by-second interest rates?
- How should we value goods and services and their relative profitability when delivery may be several decades into the future, e.g. cryogenic freezing of humans for regeneration at some unknown point in the future?

The emergence of new technology-enabled markets, commercial concepts, business models, and delivery mechanisms gives accounting firms the opportunity to embrace this new world thinking and achieve exponential growth in revenues: To win requires a change in mindsets and the investment of time and energy to really understand the new generation of technologies and what they can make possible. This also means unleashing younger generations of talent in the firm who are growing up digital and very aware of the potential prizes on offer. There is no doubt these opportunities are already emerging, and many firms will be able to capitalize on them. The choice is whether we want to be at the party, or reading about it after the event.

- *What will it take for your firm to be among the winners when we write the history of the next five years?*
- *How should we balance the effort required to drive the necessary internal changes with those required to pursue opportunities emerging from transformations in the marketplace?*
- *How can we strategize and plan for an economic system not yet created?*

A version of this article was originally published in *CCH Daily* under the title "Artificial Intelligence and the exponential growth opportunity for accounting firms."

Designing for a Post-Job Future: The Impact of AI on Architecture

By Rohit Talwar and Alexandra Whittington

What are the implications for architectural design of a world that may have fewer jobs?

All the discussion surrounding the impact of artificial intelligence (AI) on jobs raises the question: What could dramatic shifts in employment patterns mean for the built environment? Firstly, a significant proportion of the built environment has up to now been designed for people-centered economic activities—offices, shopping centers, banks, factories, and schools. Over the next 10-20 years, these may house 50% or less of the number of current workers with far fewer physical customers. Furthermore, with the rise of AI, some organizations might run on algorithms alone, with literally no human staff.

The future of jobs is not just about employment, but also about larger societal shifts with dramatic impact on the use of space and resources. Indeed, AI is increasingly likely to provide a meta-level management layer, collating data from a range of sources to monitor and control every aspect of the built environment and the use of resources within it.

Today, at the dawn of the AI revolution, some of the latest technology coming at us involves mixed reality. There is a buzz about how we can apply advances in virtual reality (VR) and augmented reality (AR) in places of work, education, and various commercial settings. Teaching and training are exemplary uses, enabling dangerous, rare, or just everyday situations to be simulated for trainees. Such simulations also provide the nexus point for humans to work alongside AI. For example, robot surgeons might do the cutting, while a human surgeon looks on remotely via video or a VR/AR interface. How might places be redesigned to accommodate this human-AI hybrid job future? The outcome could be spaces that embrace the blurring of physical and digital worlds, possibly with multi-sensory connection points between the two.

The coming waves of AI in business and society could impact the future design, use, and management of buildings in dramatic ways. Key design features, including construction, security, monitoring, and maintenance, could be coordinated by highly automated AI neural networks. For example, future office buildings might make intelligent responses to their inhabitants' moods or feelings to increase productivity of humans in the organization—varying lighting, temperature, background music, ambient smells, and digital wallpaper displays according to the motivational needs of each worker.

In the post-work, "shared infrastructure economy," architects could also factor in "multi-purposing" in the design of new buildings and the remodeling of existing ones. For example, why couldn't schools double as courtrooms, doctor's meeting rooms, social centers, and libraries in the evenings and during holidays? Empty space could become more and more of a liability to towns and cities as retail and education move online. In the US, up to 1,000 retail outlets a week are currently being closed. In response, a Texas firm has suggested a design for old shopping malls and retail outlets as drone ports, for example. Other options might include repurposing them as maker spaces, community centers, pop-up cafes, and adult learning outlets. The pace of automation of retail and commerce is likely to be exponential: Imagine a chatbot that could coordinate drone deliveries of the groceries ordered by web-connected smart refrigerators that run on IBMs Watson AI platform. Intuitive and predictive AI seems set to revolutionize the home and business.

As advances in the cognitive sciences accelerate, there is growing fascination with the idea of neuro-architecture as control mechanism in a post-work society: Will mass automation and efficiency expectations justify the construction of buildings that are responsive to people's needs, read their moods, use biometrics, and conduct behavior-conditioning of employees? There are many reasons to think these strategies could become accepted practice. Many AI analysts argue that, rather than compete with robots, humans will do more meaningful and important work than ever. Hence, the use of building design to evoke certain feelings, enhance moods and creativity, and the use of behavioral insights to motivate the workforce could provide an important advantage in the new "cobot" normal of humans working alongside intelligent robots.

As work becomes automated, it also becomes more cloud-based, and fewer offices need the amount of space they once did or for the purposes space once served. New uses of space to accommodate virtual AI workers and to provide a comfortable environment for human employees will be in demand. Furthermore, replacing actual workers with code means the layout, design, and supplies necessary for the typical office would completely change. The role of AI in reducing the amount of people and "stuff" places must accommodate should open up considerable opportunities for building redesign.

Designing to a post-job future doesn't necessarily mean that high-tech has the advantage. There will be valuable opportunities to inject a touch of humanity to key settings where people will interact with AI—work, home, and public spaces. The rise of AI means we must consider different visions of the future where 50% or more of the workforce could be automated out of a job, and the new sectors haven't taken up all the displaced individuals. With the right perspective, positive design adjustments can help make the post-work future meaningful and more human. However, the transition will be challenging for all concerned.

- *How might retrofitted building infrastructures interact with the cutting-edge technology of newer constructions?*

- *How can we effectively incorporate AI, VR, and AR into built environments?*
- *How might the design and construction of offices, houses, schools, and stores be altered by the post-job society?*

A version of this article was originally published in *Blueprint Magazine* under the title "Rohit Talwar: what does AI mean for the future of architecture?"

AI and the Many Possible Futures of the IT Professional

By Rohit Talwar, Steve Wells, and Alexandra Whittington

For IT professionals, could artificial intelligence represent the beginning of the end, or herald the dawning of a new era of opportunity?

Part of our job as futurists is to help organizations and individuals envisage how the forces shaping the future could deliver different future outcomes and to identify possible implications and action options within each scenario. There are many views of the future when it comes to artificial intelligence (AI) in the workplace and how it might impact the role of IT professionals in particular. Opinions and forecasts vary widely, with some suggesting the loss of 80% of all jobs to automation within 20 years, and others forecasting 50% employment growth over the period. Within IT, some predict developer roles could be replaced by AI within a decade, while others suggest IT could be the biggest global profession by 2030.

The reality is that no one knows—we are far too early in the evolution and application of AI to know how far and how fast it could spread and how society will react. So, rather than obsessing on predictions and forecasts, we prefer to prepare for a range of outcomes by looking at possible scenarios, and we use these future stories to highlight critical challenges and choices ahead that society needs to start preparing for today. We particularly like to focus on identifying opportunities to use technology to enhance humanity and help unleash human talent in the workplace. In this article we ask: How might AI impact IT work in the coming years?

To explore possible futures of the IT profession and its role in business, below we explore scenarios from 2019, 2021, 2023, and 2025.

IT Assignment 2019: Help Clients Differentiate Between Narrow and Deep AI

A potential IT "growth role" in 2019 might involve advising clients who have rushed the deployment of AI service software to cut costs and offended many customers in the process of doing so. For example, an unhappy internal client holds IT responsible, but the IT expert helps explain it wasn't the algorithm, but its application that offended customers. Accustomed to receiving personal messages from the organization, customers felt the automated communications were growing impersonal and showed a lack of understanding of their needs.

A key issue was that the AI wasn't trained to answer customers' questions adequately, and couldn't tell if the caller hand hung up because their query had been answered or if they had grown tired of being misunderstood. The IT professional's role here is to help clients understand when to apply deep AI (i.e. fully trained, continuously learning, customer service bots) versus narrow AI (simple, task-oriented algorithms). This type of opportunity could grow quite rapidly as AI tools become affordable for even the smallest of firms.

IT Assignment 2021: Disrupt C-Suite Hierarchies

By 2021, AI may have become so pervasive in business that it underpins every major strategy and operational decision. This could mean front-line IT staff being involved across every aspect of the business—guiding on options to achieve desired business outcomes at speed, and then developing or configuring the solutions. From start-ups to multinationals, future organizations might run on an ecosystem of AI applications, which will enhance the status of IT workers and also call on them to use a diversity of skills and talents to get the job done, including people skills and management abilities. With that said, the knife cuts both ways: CEOs and other management professionals will have to become more tech-savvy, and their roles will also encroach into the IT space. We could well see hybrid roles emerging with marketers trained to configure AI tools in the same way as they develop and run spreadsheets today.

IT Assignment 2023: Learn and Develop New Skill Sets

By 2023, in this scenario, software, hardware, and most devices are self-monitoring, self-diagnosing, and self-healing. Innovations in 3D and 4D printing make it possible to design and repair your own machine (or have it fix itself), and have made IT more organic and personalized to each customer. Open sourced AI and blockchains are being used to sprout businesses entirely absent of workers.

These distributed autonomous organizations (DAOs) run entirely on algorithms alone, with all transactions completed using smart, self-executing contracts. These companies only call in IT specialists should the AI systems fail. Automation of IT work is the norm and most white-collar jobs have disappeared. In this future, IT professionals must learn and develop new skills for the post-work world. One possible new job role would involve teaching. Not only will AI require a great deal of training, it will also drive teaching opportunities: teaching people about AI, how to work with AI, how to apply AI, and even teaching AI how to interact with people.

IT Assignment 2025: Create a Very Human Workplace

In this scenario, the world of 2025 is very different for IT professionals. In this future, most jobs have been automated, and many human workers have been replaced. However, in the face of ubiquitous and somewhat omnipotent future technologies, some IT pros have evolved their offerings. Future IT firms might focus on helping clients learn when not to use technology. At times, the IT consultant may advise that it would be in the best interest of the organization to unplug. Going offline is considered a luxury item in 2017; by 2025, with AI pushing productivity through the roof, disconnecting could be the key to sanity.

An example IT requirement in 2025 might be to put the organization on an "information vacation" where employees can put work aside to socialize, connect, and reinvigorate relationships face to face. Recognizing when not to use technology may become a key function of healthy businesses, giving IT a natural leadership role in creating a very human workplace.

Scenarios aren't exhaustive representations of the future, but necessary wake up calls. Studying and creating diverse images of the future are an insurance policy of sorts against future surprises. Is it probable that by 2025 the main value-add of IT services will be its ability to shut off the technology? No. But it is a provocative image that drives home the idea that technology is not the enemy, but a highly malleable tool that works at our disposal, and its role in the workplace is up to us to decide.

- *Could increased digital literacy, coupled with smarter development tools, turn every employee into an IT expert?*
- *What skills might enable IT professionals to transition into executive and strategy roles across departments?*
- *How might these changes in the profession impact the training and education IT professionals need to receive?*

A version of this article was originally published in *ITProPortal* under the title "AI and the many future of futures of the IT Professional."

Artificial Intelligence – The Next Frontier in IT Security?

By April Koury and Rohit Talwar

How might AI impact future developments in cyber security?

Security has always been an arms race between attacker and defender. He starts a war with a stick, you get a spear; he counters with a musket, you upgrade to a cannon; he develops a tank, you split the atom. While the consequences of organizational cybersecurity breaches may not be as earth-shatteringly dramatic today, the centuries-old arms race continues into the digital sphere of today.

The next challenge for companies with an eye towards the future should be to recognize that artificial intelligence (AI) is already entering the scene. For example, we are seeing the emergence of AI tools like PatternEx—focused on spotting cyberattacks—and Feedzai for fraud detection across the ecommerce value chain. The technology is developing so rapidly that it is too early to say whether the impact will be revolutionary, or just the next evolution in the continued digital age cybersecurity arms race.

Artificial Intelligence
Some AI evangelists argue this new technological force could render all others seemingly irrelevant given the scale of change, risk, and

opportunity it could bring about in IT security. This new dark art offering seemingly magical technological wizardry does indeed have the potential to change our world, and—depending on who you choose to believe—either make life a little better, lead to total societal transformation, or end humanity itself.

As a result of a new generation of disruptive technologies coupled with AI, we are entering the Fourth Industrial Revolution. The three previous revolutions gave us steam-based mechanization, electrification, and mass production, followed by electronics, information technology, and automation. This new fourth era, with its smart machines, is fueled by exponential improvement and convergence of multiple scientific and technological fields into an all-encompassing Internet of things (IoT). The medium to long-term outcomes of these converging exponential technologies for individuals, society, business, government, and IT security are far from clear.

The pace of AI development is accelerating and astounding even those in the sector. In March 2016, Google DeepMind's AlphaGo system beat the world GO champion—demonstrating the speed of development taking place in machine learning, a core AI technology. The board game GO has billions of possible moves; you cannot teach the system all the rules and permutations. Instead, AlphaGo was equipped with a machine learning algorithm that enabled it to deduce the rules and possible moves from observing thousands of games. Its successor AlphaGo Zero taught itself to play GO in three days without observing any human games and then beat AlphaGo by 100 games to nil. This same technology can now be used in IT security in applications ranging from external threat detection and prevention to spotting the precursors of potentially illegal behavior amongst employees.

The Current State of Affairs in IT Security

In 2015 in the US, the Identity Theft Resource Center noted that almost 180 million personal records were exposed to data breaches, and a PwC survey report highlighted that 79% of responding US organizations had experienced at least one security incident. Industry research indicates that while hackers exploit vulnerabilities within minutes of their becoming known, companies take roughly 146 days to fix critical vulnerabilities. With the average cost of a data breach estimated at US$4 million, there is growing concern over how companies can keep up with the constant onslaught of ever stealthier, faster, and malicious attacks today and in the future.

As it stands, many firms focus more on reacting to security breaches rather than preventing them, and the current approach to network security is often aimed more at "standards compliance" rather than detecting new and evolving threats. The result is an unwinnable game of whack-a-mole that could overwhelm companies in the future unless they are willing to adopt and adapt the mindset, technology, and techniques used by the hackers. And there is very little doubt that hackers are—or soon will be—developing AI tools to increase the frequency, scale, breadth, and sophistication of their attacks.

Organizations in this digital age create infinite amounts of data, both internally through their own processes and externally via customers, suppliers, and partners. No one human can analyze all that data to monitor for potential security breaches—our systems have simply become too widespread, data-laden, and unwieldy. However, when combined with big data management tools, AI is becoming ever more effective at crunching vast amounts of data and picking out patterns and anomalies. In fact, with most AI systems, the more information they are fed, the smarter they become.

AI's Future Potential

One of the biggest potential security benefits of AI lies in detecting internal threats. Imagine an AI system that, day in and day out, watches the comings and goings of all employees within a corporate headquarters via biometrics and login information. It knows, for example, that the CFO normally logs out of the cloud each day by 12 noon and heads to the company gym, where she spends an average of 45 minutes. One day it spots an anomaly—the CFO has logged into the cloud at 12:20 pm. is intelligent enough to compare her location with this unexpected login—according to its data, the CFO's face was last scanned on entering the gym and has not been seen leaving the gym, but the cloud login originated from her office.

The AI recognizes the anomaly, correlates the discrepancy between login and CFO locations, shuts down cloud access to the CFO's account, and begins defensive measures against potential cyberattacks. The system also alerts the CFO, and escalates this high priority problem to human cybersecurity within seconds. Important company data and financial records are safe thanks to AI security. Imagine how its capabilities will grow as this same AI system continues to learn from and predict the behavior of hundreds or hundreds of thousands of employees across the organization—helping it monitor for and predict similar security breaches.

Beyond employee behavior, our AI security application is also watching the company's internal systems and learning how they interact. It discovers when customer information is added into the company's database, accounting software automatically picks up the information and an invoice is generated within an average of 7.5 seconds. Any deviation outside of normal behavior by .25 seconds triggers the AI to investigate every link within the process and tease out the cause. In this case, based on what it discovers (an inconsequential lag in the system), the AI security properly prioritizes the incident as a nonthreatening low risk, but will continue to monitor for similar lags and alert system maintenance to the issue just in case.

Now let's take this scenario a step further—imagine that not only has this AI system learned the behavior of hundreds of employees and of the internal company networks, but it is also capable of continually learning from external cyberattacks. The more cyberattacks thrown at the AI, the more data it can parse, and like a thinking, rational soldier who has manned the battlements through numerous campaigns, the better educated and prepared it becomes for future attacks. It will recognize totally new, hostile code based on experience and previous exposure to related patterns of attack behavior. It will build defenses as it works to unravel the new hostile code, and as the offensive AI code attempts to adapt to the new defenses, the AI security will continually develop new methods to counter and destroy the invader.

This is the potential AI security system of the near future—fully integrated inside and out, noninvasive to daily business, and always on alert and ready to defend. It will be the ultimate digital sentry—hopefully learning and adapting as quickly as the attackers.

Organizations' Approach to AI Security

Just as the stick fight eventually escalated to nuclear weapons, so too will the AI battle between organizations and hackers keep evolving. Continual one-upmanship will become the norm in AI security, perhaps to the point where even developers will be unable to decipher the exact workings of their constantly learning and evolving security algorithms. As complex and expensive as this all sounds, will companies in the future, especially smaller organizations, be able to survive without AI?

As the stakes become higher and failures loom larger, ever evolving AI threats may encourage far more collaboration across multiple companies. Smaller organizations could band together under one AI security system, dispersing the cost and maintenance across multiple payers, while larger players with the financial and technological muscle to own their own AI security may exchange critical information on cyberattacks—or rather, their AIs could exchange information on cyberattacks and learn from each other.

Alternatively, companies could become so overwhelmed that they simply opt for simple, technologically cheaper "brute force" non-AI solutions to counter increasingly complex AI hacks. The simple, or dumb, solution may entail more checks and passwords across accounts and devices, or perhaps security enhanced devices that are changed every two weeks. While adding five layers of complex passwords to any login or continuously rotating through smart phones could protect company security, the increased overhead, employee frustration, and time wasted with cumbersome security measures would not be seen as ideal and could hinder the firm's reputation—which might make it more susceptible to attack.

While an AI system will quietly monitor security and enable

employees to focus on their work, the simple non-AI solution will place an unnecessary security burden on the employees—they will be responsible for keeping up with those five complex passwords and changing devices on a biweekly basis. Whereas the AI system is maintained by a few cybersecurity experts, the simple security solution is in the hands of every employee, vastly multiplying the chances of a security breach. In the future, this simple non-AI solution might become a defensive strategy of survival rather than an adaptive offensive campaign of a leading, thriving business.

The Role of Humans in AI Security

Of course, at this point a natural question is, "If AI is quicker, smarter, and continually adapting to do its job better, why even bother with human cybersecurity?" Today, AI security must still learn from humans, and although it may one day reach the point where it no longer requires expert involvement, that day remains at least a few years down the road. Furthermore, depending on how valuable we deem human oversight and intuition in security, that day may never come to pass. AI security systems currently need humans to write their starter algorithms, and provide the necessary data, training, and feedback to guide their learning. Humans are currently an essential part of the deployment of AI, and as AI security evolves beyond this nascent stage, the role for humans in AI will evolve as well.

As organizations increasingly digitize processes, amassing mind-boggling amounts of sensitive data, new importance will be placed on the role of the human architects and minders of AI security systems. Never has so much data been so easily accessible to attack, and even small attacks gathering seemingly innocuous data could add up to catastrophic security breaches. Developers of AI security will become akin to nuclear weapons inspectors in importance—highly trustworthy individuals who have undergone extensive background checks and intensive training, vetting, and accreditation. They will not only build AI security, but also provide oversight and intuitive guidance in the training process and be an integral line of cybersecurity defense.

AI security will go far beyond human capabilities, freeing organizations and cybersecurity experts from the impossible task of constant vigilance, allowing them to prevent future attacks without interrupting daily workflow. Tomorrow's AI security system will learn, self-improve, and run discreetly behind the scenes—intelligently monitoring, prioritizing, and destroying threats; ever evolving into the next finely-honed weapon in the cybersecurity armory.

- *Where does cybersecurity in the AI age sit on your organization's priority list?*
- *Will SME's be able to survive without AI security in the future?*
- *Could we see corporations increasingly resorting to cyberattacks as a means of gaining competitive advantage?*

A version of this article was originally published in *Network Security Journal*.

IMPACTS OF AI ON BUSINESS

Artificial Intelligence in the Workplace - The Leadership Challenge

AI - Addressing the Human and Workplace Implications

Hope is Not a Strategy - Retention, Engagement, and Productivity in the Era of Artificial Intelligence

Small Business and AI: Now, Next, and Future

Artificial Intelligence in the Workplace – The Leadership Challenge

By Rohit Talwar, Steve Wells, and Alexandra Whittington

How might the nature of leadership change as AI takes on an increasing role in the workplace?

Introduction

Technological disruptions are defining this era of rapid business transformation and driving a set of deep-rooted questions about the future of work, the implications for organizations, management, and employees, and how we can navigate to the "next horizon." On a near daily basis we hear questions such as:

- How might humans work with artificial intelligence (AI) and robots?
- What tasks will AI take from humans and what might we then focus on?
- How quickly might change happen?
- What skills will we need to manage an environment populated by people and smart machines?
- Could smart technology become our line manager or lead our organizations?

- How might tomorrow's workplace evolvedue to these changes?

This article explores these questions and the different possible scenarios that could emerge in a world where our reality and sense of the possible is being redefined on a daily basis.

The Fourth Industrial Revolution

The revolutions of the past—steam-based mechanization, electronics, and information technology—are being surpassed by a new fourth era of smart machine-enabled transformation. How businesses respond to the challenges and exploit the benefits of smart technologies such as AI will be a key determinant of success going forward.

Technological developments are starting to change the nature, scope, and scale of work; traditional business models are being overturned, professional roles are changing, and whole industry sectors are being reinvented or created anew. We single out AI as perhaps the most disruptive technology fueling this radical transformation.

Where Do We See AI Going in the Next Five Years?

AI combined with the Internet of things (IoT) is already giving rise to the new world of smart cities, where the physical infrastructure gathers and feeds back data via the cloud to inform planning, service provision, and even policing. This coupled with AI in autonomous vehicles (AVs) will lead to a new category of self-owning assets including buildings and public infrastructure. Vehicles may change from being unused resource drains, sitting idle for most of their lives, to sources of income. An AV may be able to go out to work for you, earning a supplementary income or own itself and share the revenues with its manufacturer, servicer, and refueler.

The power of AI to gather massive amounts of data, analyze, interpret, draw inferences, and make predictions has applications in every industry sector. Smart infrastructure, powered by AI and linked to the IoT, could revolutionize estates and facilities departments. For example, we may see the rise of smart hospitals, where all types of resources, from medicines and medical equipment to the actual fabric of the hospital—beds, walls, and partitions—are deployed where necessary based on AI predictive analytics. We may see a time when an AI is running an entire hospital.

Task automation is a key area for AI applications. Roles that have been traditionally thought of as requiring a high level human intellect are now being automated. The legal profession is seeing such disruption: Legal precedent and case review can be automated, contracts can be created and adapted, case outcomes can be predicted, and workload can be organized by an AI.

As task automation becomes commonplace and increasingly applied to chatbots or social media output, simple query responses and content delivery in social channels are being delivered by AI. Whilst it boosts efficiency, decision makers must be mindful of how this type of task automation may impact brand identity and user experience, and where it is still critical to maintain human involvement. As similar smart automation is deployed by competing businesses, there's a risk of commoditization—and how firms stand out and maintain personality will be a critical consideration. The challenge is deploying the technology to unleash human potential and take our businesses to the next level, rather than simply automating what we do to reduce costs.

The structure of entire businesses may be revolutionized: For example, the number of decentralized autonomous organizations (DAOs) is growing; these organizations exist entirely in software and therefore require no human employees. Currently, DAOs exist in a hinterland—it is as yet unclear what their legal status is, and this in itself raises questions as to how we perceive a business. In the near future, as DAOs may increase in prevalence, questions will be raised over the necessity for human involvement and influence in business at all.

All these areas of potential disruption evidence the growing need to focus on the human dimension. How will staff respond when their jobs are drastically changed or eliminated? How will we mitigate worries or stress that AI may cause? What new skills might employees need? What responsibilities do employers have for those displaced by technology? Some analysts estimate that 80% of current jobs could disappear within 20 years, and others project that for each job created in new firms and sectors, three will be eliminated elsewhere.

Leadership Priorities

So, what do leaders need to understand and pay attention to as their organization embarks on the AI journey?

Deep and Narrow Applications of AI

An initial consideration is how deep to deploy AI within a business as it has both deep and narrow applications; AI can be used narrowly to automate a single task or apply rule-based thinking to a process or outcome, or it may be used to automate entire departments, e.g. customer service. How deep to take AI will depend on the goals, priorities, resources, and values of the firm and where it sees the place of humans in service, innovation, and sales.

Hierarchies Disrupted

It may be natural to think that the IT department should lead the way in driving adoption of AI across the business; however, the increasingly strategic nature of the decisions embedded in the choice to deploy AI may be sitting more in the realm of the COO, CEO, or heads of business units and functions. Importantly, the learning to support these leadership decisions can be drawn from a multitude of different places: Industry associations, conferences, and networking events, can facilitate learning and networking opportunities, and vendors can share their experience and advice. Furthermore, discussions with other organizations who've experimented with AI can allow us to tap into their knowledge and experience, and science and technology graduates can intern to bring technical expertise and fresh perspectives to a firm in exchange for business experience.

A Very Human Workplace

There is a growing risk that firms will become over-reliant on technology and ignore the value of humans. Smart technology will increasingly replace even complex roles. It will be some time, however, before technology can outperform humans in problem solving, creativity, negotiation, collaborative design, conflict resolution, and crisis response. Digital transformation initiatives typically fail as a result of paying too little attention to the human and cultural aspects of change and their place in the future solution. Hence, we need to think about how to invest in staff to maximize their potential with technology in an enabling role; how to care for those whose roles and departments are being disrupted by AI; and how to raise everyone's digital literacy so they understand the nature of the technology that is bringing about such change in their world.

Training may be necessary to facilitate the transition to working in an AI-centric firm, something akin to cultural or sensitivity training to allow employees to become accustomed to the new technology. HR may have a greater role to play in professional development: For example, a senior manager whose job is being fundamentally disrupted for the first time in their career may need a degree of retraining and emotional support.

New Skill Sets

As AI becomes commonplace, employees' soft skills will become even more important. As rule-based thinking and automation proliferate in businesses, skills like sensitivity, creativity, verbal reasoning, communication, empathy, and spontaneity may be increasingly desirable. HR or a new Department of Humanity can facilitate this aspect of personal development to ensure that businesses make the most of the interplay between personal and artificial intelligence.

Striking a Fine Balance

Importantly, firms of all sizes and in all sectors will need to strike a fine balance between AI and the human workforce in their organizations. To preserve the human element of your business in an automated climate, what will act as a key differentiator? Careful decisions about which roles and functions to automate should guide AI strategy in business—a simple "bottom line" approach will compromise the human element and could erode the firm's uniqueness over time. It will also be important to show compassion and support to employees displaced by new technology.

The gifts from AI to society include smarter decision making and the capacity to draw new insights from vast arrays of data. There is also the potential for cost-saving replacement of humans, and for efficiency-oriented high-volume applications which are simply beyond human capacity to execute in a meaningful timeframe, e.g. scanning literally millions of websites in an information search. However, a sweeping implementation of AI without regard for the impact on employees would be bad internal PR at the least, and could have devastating consequences in terms of customer appeal and local reputation for a business. Furthermore, the cost of widespread unemployment cannot be carried by the public alone; private industry will almost certainly be expected to contribute to a solution to the economic instability that rash automation would create.

Voluntary programs to address the impact on communities might be a consideration. Options organizations might consider would include supporting universal basic income (UBI) policies and programs for workers displaced by technology. Employers can also assist with local new business creation programs and adult retraining initiatives. In the longer-term future, some governments may compel companies to do so—might some jurisdictions apply an AI/robot/automation tax to private companies to fund the resulting unemployment benefit and retraining costs? Organizations might also offer a form of pension designed around the phased automation of jobs, knowing certain work will be performed by AI in five to ten years. A spin-off industry that might emerge could be a form of income insurance that workers could purchase to protect themselves from future automation, with the funds invested directly in the providers of the technologies that will be replacing the humans. Whilst disruption will create threats, there are also significant opportunities that the deployment of AI in business could deliver.

The Future of Work Has Already Begun

Ultimately the future of work and the future of society are deeply entwined. Our sense of place in society, our worth, our contribution, and our legacy are often predicated around our work. Anything that starts to disrupt that relationship between work and individual identity is going to have far-reaching impacts. On the plus side, humans have proved themselves to be remarkably adaptable. So, while the idea of working side-by-side with a robot may at first be unsettling, a small step back reminds us that we already work and relate with AI and "smart" machines every day. For example, predictive text is a form of AI software to which most smartphone users have adjusted.

When sending emails or texts on devices, or running an internet search, we expect, to some extent, that our intention will be perceived. Advertising, too, has become so personalized via monitoring of our browsing and social media patterns that we expect to see the products we like and want pitched to us—their absence could signal that something might be wrong with the security of the device. Putting aside personal annoyances with advertisements and predictive text (for certain, many smartphone users have deactivated these "features"), they are a subtle reminder that the everyday machines we trust with our pictures, contacts, passwords, location, and sometimes a biometric identifier or two, are learning about us in ways that could both help us and potentially invade our privacy in undesirable ways.

The AI companions that will join us in the workforce will be preoccupied with learning about us to try to make our lives better. Just as the predictive text on your phone doesn't send runaway messages (usually) and the internet search bar sometimes knows you better than you know yourself, society should anticipate AI's helpful (if sometimes at first clunky) role in the workplace over the coming decade.

- *What values should we be emphasizing to ensure workplaces retain a very human quality?*
- *Could AI lead to higher expectations for interpersonal encounters in the workplace?*
- *What kind of relationship might employees and clients want with AI?*

AI – Addressing the Human and Workplace Implications

An Interview with Steve Wells, Rohit Talwar, and Alexandra Whittington

How might the next wave of AI impact the workplace?

How far has the use of AI in the workplace come in the last five years?

In the last five years the stage has been set for what's being called the Fourth Industrial Revolution. The technological ability to compute at the scale and speed needed for widespread artificial intelligence (AI) has been achieved. At the same time, the rise of cloud-based digital services via Amazon and Google have essentially outsourced AI and put the technology in reach of even the smallest of organizations. This levelling of the playing field has been a core benefit of technology shifts in the last five years, and is a key reason why we're about to see an exponential rise in the implementation of AI in the workplace— everywhere from retail to law firms—and in activities ranging from sales and service to product design, finance, and HR.

How is it currently being used in businesses? In what forms and ways?

Research from McKinsey suggests that:

- Less than 5% of jobs can be fully automated by adapting

currently demonstrated technology—up to 20% for middle-skill categories;[1]

- 60% of jobs have at least 30% of activities that are technically automatable, based on current technologies;[2]
- Automation technologies could affect 49% of the world economy—1.1 billion employees and $12.7 trillion in wages;[3]
- 47% of workers in the USA have jobs at high risk of potential automation; 35% in the UK, 49% in Japan.[4]

It depends very much on the sector, but in a general sense, tools such as WorkFusion are being used to break high volume, complex data processing, and analysis work into discrete tasks and algorithmically assign them to appropriate machine and human resources. Such platforms look to improve human productivity by leveraging a combination of internal, outsourced, and crowdsourced workers. Users control which types of workers contribute to externally crowdsourced work. The software learns a broader range of activities from its human counterparts and extends the scale and complexity of what it can handle. Over time, humans are engaged only when algorithms face new obstacles or challenges for any task.

Wearable devices such as health and fitness trackers are increasing in power and popularity and gradually becoming part of the workforce management toolset. These wristbands and tags can be worn as fashion accessories and monitor multiple aspects of health and fitness. It seems inevitable that some employees will be required to wear these devices as a condition of employment, while others may expect employers to provide them.

How are these disruptive technologies affecting people's jobs?

Here are some key trends that have caught our attention recently:

- Gartner estimates that by 2018, two million employees will be required to wear health and fitness tracking devices as a condition of employment.
- Tractica predicts more than 75 million wearables will permeate the workplace by 2020.

- A PWC survey found 49% believe wearable tech will increase workplace efficiency, while 37% expect their company to adopt the latest technology even if it doesn't directly influence their work.
- 67% of consumers said that employers should pay for their device.
- Only 25% of respondents said they would not trust any company with personal information associated with wearable technology.

These insights point to an evolution in the relationship between employees and employers centered on the right to use personal data, purpose, and trust, all of which are more important than ever in the workplace and essential to any sane rollout of AI in the workplace. To retain credibility, it seems essential that employers express openness and transparency around the use of their people's personal information.

Chatbots have been used in customer services for many years but are now being used for other functions such as coaching and in HR to answer general employee queries—where do you see this progress going in the future?

Future chat bots will use AI to become increasingly intuitive and predict customers' needs and wants before they express them. This ability to make decisions for us, particularly the ones that can be made on our history, is one of the key promises of AI. It's also the thing which could potentially make us lazy and stupid—not having to think for ourselves, so it's a double-edged sword. So, for example, in the future, you might not have to really read over and understand different employee benefit plans. Your personal AI might decide for you. It would be a convenience, but it would also involve turning over a lot of trust to what's basically just a computer program—the same one that performs autocorrect on your phone. Would you trust it to negotiate your salary, decide on which employee benefits to choose, and make other important HR decisions on your behalf? The technology hasn't yet reached that point, nor has the level of trust between humans and technology.

Can you remove the human element completely?

Not for some time. However, although we can expect to see more and more such organizations run entirely by code in the future, and they will have no people—no bosses or workers whatsoever. There are already live examples of this type of company, called a distributed autonomous organization (DAO). For example, one is currently set up as an investment fund to allow for digital currency owners to vote with their invested currency on start-up/investment ideas. The company then executes the investment and recoups the investors' rewards through a series of smart contracts.

We can expect to see many more DAOs in the future, some running with a combination of smart contracts and AI, but there will still have to be a human element behind it. Once AI gets to the point where it can write its own code, we may have to make stronger safeguards to keep it from, say, investing against the votes. A lot of people lost money on a DAO a year or so ago—it wasn't because the technology went haywire, but good old-fashioned human crime. We will still need to protect against that.

Looking ahead, will they replace or merely reconfigure the role of the HR function?

We are heading into a world that will require not "Ordinary Management," but "Extraordinary Leadership." The leadership and management style required when working in uncertain situations can be challenging. For "Ordinary Management" we apply accepted best practice approaches; it's the domain of tame problems and technical challenges. But in the increasingly disruption-filled world we are heading into, we require "Extraordinary Leadership," where tasks are sometimes difficult or impossible to complete because of incomplete, contradictory, and changing requirements that are often difficult to reconcile or even recognize.

Determining the organizational capacity to work in new ways— envisioning the future and making sense of complexity – seem to be critical tasks for HR to take control of. The challenge is to explore different ways that AI could enhance and complement humanity, rather than overshadow and form a threat to prosperity. There are several authors whom we've interviewed and talked to in depth about the future of HR, and the actual extent that robots will take jobs is highly debatable.

Even among the world's foremost experts, there's no real agreement as we are at such an early stage in the evolution of smart automation—will robots take 10% of jobs? 50%? 70%—or create 30% more? We don't yet know. That is why we use scenarios, for example, to explore the future of AI in business: Telling different stories of possible futures helps us wrap our heads around a very big picture. Visualizing the different possible outcomes is one of the most valuable parts of our foresight work and our books and articles. It helps to articulate the drivers, the fears, the possibilities, and the risks. Understanding different possible trajectories helps organizations make more robust choices and move forward.

Some of the key questions arising for leaders include:

- How can we create a generationally and technologically diverse culture?
- How can we drive culture change that aligns with evolving business propositions for evolving customers?
- Does Human Resources need to transition to Resource Management and adopt a more business–wide strategic role to match all the resource options—human or otherwise—to meet the organization's business objectives?
- Chatbots are one manifestation of AI—what other things can we expect to see, particularly with regards to HR, but also other process-driven departments, such as IT and accounts?

Personal AI assistants that operate as a sort of "digital twin" may be on the horizon—these constantly learning assistants would be an algorithmic stand-in for any given worker in terms of having access to and knowledge of their behaviors, assumptions, calendars, customers, projects, and contacts. This would be a highly valuable innovation in HR because it would essentially double the workforce by cloning every employee "in the cloud." This would allow for much more effective training, transfer of knowledge, and transparency across the organization. It would also require a considerable amount of trust from employee to employer. Can we trust our employers to essentially hack into our brains and possess whatever exists inside that they deem theirs? Although AI is likely to be increasingly cheap and ubiquitous in 10 to 20 years, human brilliance may become a rare and nonrenewable resource.

Additionally, brain scanning technologies are already in place to monitor rising and falling emotion levels, concentration, and productivity. If used properly and ethically, these technologies could present HR with new opportunities to truly monitor workforce health and well-being. Data collected from wearables and brain monitors could be analyzed using AI to enable continual performance feedback.

- *What conversations is your organization having about the extent to which it wants to pursue AI in the workplace?*
- *What does your business see as its responsibility towards those displaced by automation?*
- *How can we retain the capacity for free thinking, creativity, and problem solving when standardized and automated thinking is becoming the prevailing mindset?*

A version of this article was originally published in *People Management*.

Hope is Not a Strategy – Retention, Engagement, and Productivity in the Era of Artificial Intelligence

By Rohit Talwar, Steve Wells, April Koury, Alexandra Whittington, and Maria Romero

With regular warnings that technologies such as artificial intelligence will replace most of the workforce, what could this mean for the future of employee retention, engagement, and productivity?

Artificial intelligence (AI) is the latest manifestation of a techno-logical revolution that started over a century ago. Each phase of workplace revolution has stirred things up and disrupted jobs and the way they are rewarded. This time round is no exception, and the smart machines of this Fourth Industrial Revolution open up new possibilities for how we employ, engage, motivate, retain, and reward people.

Where Do We See AI Going?
As a result of AI and related exponentially advancing technologies such as cloud computing, new industry sectors are emerging, old ones are being disrupted, business models are being upturned, and workplaces and the nature of work are being reinvented. As a result,

jobs, professional roles, management, motivation, and rewards are all being revisited to ensure they are relevant to the next world of work. Whilst disruption creates threats, there are also significant opportunities emerging in relation to employee retention, engagement, and productivity.

Employee Retention
With a life expectancy of 110 or more for today's 11-year-olds, the idea of lifelong employment becomes more mythical by the day. Indeed, the definition of a job as one's sole source of financial security might become obsolete sooner than we'd hope. Over time, and possibly quite rapidly, the proportion receiving universal basic income (UBI) might rise in comparison to those on salaries. We may rely increasingly on a governmental or corporate-sponsored fund that provides—potentially unconditional—cash payments to all. As employees become more sensitized to the job risks posed by automation, they could increasingly evaluate employers based on what provisions they will offer to those displaced by technology. This might include physical and mental health support, skills retraining, and assistance with small business creation.

As salaries and pensions come under threat, employees might use new criteria to size up their job prospects. For example, employers might offer to help create and maintain individuals' social media profiles and show them how to monetize their networks and generate additional income streams—for example securing advertisers for the digital screen on the back of your jacket. Employers could also aggregate the personal data of those employees who have opted in, selling it on and sharing the revenues with those employees.

One emerging possibility is that employees would get paid extra for sharing their own cognitive assets. Uploading thoughts to a digital AI cloud, even authorizing company ownership of their mind, might become one path to a raise or job security. In this sense, AI offers new ways for organizations to commit to a code of ethics; some companies might have policies against such practices, whereas others might exploit employees or practice "thought slavery," or reward such employee commitment generously. The company ethics guiding the use of AI in the workplace could determine the attractiveness of a place to work or invest in.

Employee Engagement

We've all seen the comedy caricatures of tech firms where the employee literally gives their soul to the firm—available 24/7, participating in firm-sponsored social activities, and being a total "brand ambassador." With AI, this becomes more of a reality, with the technology in the workplace and on our phones monitoring every aspect of our engagement from the words we use to our purchase of rival brands.

The use of AI also means the future of employment may involve benefits unlike anything available today.

In this potentially disturbing future, insurance companies might look at a person's data and digital assets as commodities; with so much transparency being provided by AI and the vast data it can amass and analyze, risk could become obsolete. We could literally predict every activity, choice, and outcome down to the most likely time, cause, and place of death. Health benefit providers would think differently since they could proactively monitor health and other behavioral factors. Furthermore, in the absence of cash from a steady life-long job, people could trade their own data to extract value from it, like borrowing from a pension. With AI, employee benefits should become more personalized—for example taking rewards in the form of discount vouchers and personal services.

Employee Productivity

With AI, some expect economic productivity to skyrocket. This is the main appeal to companies, of course, in the sense that it is much cheaper to write one algorithm than to support an office full of employees. So, will humans seek to enhance their minds and bodies to be able to compete with robots? One rather strange outcome might include enhanced employees using bionic, pharmaceutical, or digital augmentation to perform their job. Some companies might offer human augmentations, support groups, or inclusivity trainings.

Others might come up with "Augmentationships" or "Enhancement-ships" where candidates could try enhancements for a limited time. Augmentation could be an employment benefit and an attractive quality in a potential employee.

The Gifts of AI

The gifts from AI to society include smarter decision making, the capacity to draw new insights from vast arrays of data, the potential for cost-saving replacement of humans, and efficiency beyond human capacity. However, a sweeping implementation of AI without regard for the impact on employees could have devastating consequences. In the here and now, organizations might explore radical concepts like a pension designed around the phased automation of jobs, knowing certain work will be performed by AI in five to ten years. The best-case scenario is the future where AI emerges as a benefit to workers, organizations, and society; however, this requires careful planning as hope is not a strategy.

- *What sort of approach should governments and companies take towards regulating or mandating the use of human augmentations?*
- *What might a company reasonably be expected to provide as a "safety net" for its employees?*
- *How can we best teach people about the value of their data and the potential commercial uses and misuses of what they share?*

A version of this article was originally published in *Corporate Adviser.*

Small Business and AI: Now, Next, and Future

By Rohit Talwar, Steve Wells, April Koury, and Alexandra Whittington

How can small to medium enterprises prepare for and take advantage of AI?

Technological disruptions are driving our current era of rapid business transformation and raising questions about what the future of work might be, the implications for organizations, and how to navigate successfully to the "next horizon." How small businesses respond to the challenges and exploit the benefits of smart technologies such as artificial intelligence (AI) will be a key determinant of their success going forward.

Artificial intelligence is the rapidly growing field of computer science focused on creating intelligent software tools able to replicate critical human mental faculties. Artificial intelligence is perhaps the most disruptive technology fueling the radical transformation of business; it is truly altering the nature, scope, and scale of today's organizations. With a level of focused attention on the now, the next, and the future of AI, small business leaders will be able to prepare for a range of possible outcomes and increase their organizations' resilience in the face of future uncertainty.

The Now

Task automation is currently a key area for AI applications. Roles that have been traditionally thought of as requiring a high level of human intellect are being automated. The legal profession is seeing such disruption: Legal precedent and case review can be automated, contracts can be created and adapted, case outcomes can be predicted, and workload can be organized by an AI. Small businesses' initial consideration should be how deep to deploy AI within the organization—AI can be used narrowly to automate a single task, or it may be used to go deeper and automate entire departments, e.g. customer service. How deep to take AI will depend on the goals, priorities, and, especially, on the resources of smaller firms, and on where they see the future role of humans in service, innovation, and sales.

Additionally, whilst AI boosts efficiency, decision makers must be mindful of how this may impact brand identity and user experience, and where it is still critical to maintain human involvement. As similar levels of smart automation are deployed by competing businesses, there's a risk of commoditization: How firms stand out and maintain personality in the near future will be a critical consideration. The goal for now should be to figure out how to best deploy AI to help unleash human potential and take the business to the next level, rather than simply automate current tasks to reduce costs.

The Next

In a relatively few years, it is possible that firms may risk becoming over-reliant on AI technology while ignoring the value of human contributions in the workplace. Moreover, digital transformation initiatives typically fail because they pay too little attention to the human and cultural aspects of change. Smaller organizations will need to consider how to best invest in the technologies that will enable, not hinder staff; the challenge is how to care for those whose roles are being disrupted by AI; and how to raise everyone's digital literacy so they understand and accept the nature of this work-altering technology. Luckily for smaller organizations that may not have a dedicated IT department, the strategic nature of deploying AI company-wide may fall under the responsibilities of the COO or CEO.

Support for these organization-changing leadership decisions can be drawn from a multitude of different places: Industry associations, conferences, and events can facilitate learning and networking opportunities; vendors can share their experience and advice; discussions with other organizations who have experimented with AI can allow leaders to tap into first-hand knowledge and experience; and science and technology graduates can intern to bring technical expertise and fresh perspectives to a firm in exchange for business experience.

As AI is adopted across the organization, business leaders should be aware that different levels of training may be necessary to facilitate transition, something akin to cultural or sensitivity training, that helps employees become accustomed to the new technology. Understandably, a senior manager whose job is being fundamentally disrupted may require more retraining and emotional support than the customer service representative who was hired a month ago.

Furthermore, small business leaders need to keep in mind that a sweeping implementation of AI without regard for the impact on employees would be bad internal PR at the least, and could have devastating consequences in terms of customer appeal and local reputation for a business. Careful decisions about which roles and functions to automate should guide AI strategy in the next few years—a simple "bottom line" approach may compromise the human element and could erode the firm's uniqueness over time.

The Future

Within the foreseeable future, the structure of entire businesses may be revolutionized. For example, the number of decentralized autonomous organizations (DAOs) is growing; these organizations exist entirely in software—adopting self-executing smart contracts—and therefore require no human employees. This raises questions as to how businesses will be perceived in the future. And as DAOs increase in prevalence, will there be a need for human involvement and influence in business at all? With AI becoming commonplace, employees' soft skills will be ever more important. As rule-based thinking, automation, and DAOs proliferate, sensitivity, creativity, verbal reasoning, communication, empathy, and spontaneity may become increasingly desirable skills. Smaller businesses should encourage and facilitate these aspects of personal development to ensure that their organizations make the most of this interplay between emotional intelligence and artificial intelligence.

Finally, and somewhat contrarily, future firms might focus on learning when not to use technology. Going offline is considered a luxury in 2017; by 2025, with AI pushing productivity through the roof, disconnecting could be the key to differentiating and rehumanizing smaller firms. An organization in 2025 might enact an "information vacation" where employees could put digital work aside to socialize, connect, and reinvigorate business and client relationships face to face rather than AI assistant to AI assistant. Recognizing when not to use technology may become a key function of healthy businesses, and place smaller firms in higher standing with key clients.

Ultimately, the now, the next, and the future of AI all evidence the growing need for small businesses to focus on the human dimension. How will staff respond when their jobs are drastically changed or eliminated because of AI? How will the organization mitigate worries or stress that AI may cause? What new skills might employees need? What responsibilities does the firm have for those displaced by technology? These are the questions small business leaders should continuously ask themselves as they plan for the AI-enabled future.

- *How could AI help level the playing field for SMEs when competing with larger companies?*
- *How would we compete when AIs are able to start small businesses on their own?*
- *Who is best positioned to lead the AI effort in your company?*

A version of this article was originally published in *Bytestart*.

IMPACTS OF AI ON JOBS AND THE ECONOMY

Dancing with Disruption– 20 Jobs that Could Be Transformed by AI

By Rohit Talwar, Steve Wells, Maria Romero, and Alexandra Whittington

Will intelligent machines take, make, or reboot your job—how might AI transform occupations and professions across society?

The robots are coming—"Lock up your knowledge and protect your job at all costs!" The apocalyptic warnings are starting to flow of how artificial intelligence (AI) and robotics combined with other disruptive technologies could eliminate the need for humans in the workplace. Equally skeptical voices are rubbishing the idea that anything drastic will happen, citing previous industrial revolutions as proof that new jobs will emerge to fill any gaps created by the automation of existing ones. In practice, no one really knows how quickly AI might eliminate jobs, or what the employment needs will be of the future businesses and industries that have not yet been born.

What we do know is that AI is one of the key exponentially improving technologies shaping both the workplace of the future and the roles that will be available for humans and machines. Some forecasts suggest that by 2030, 50% or more of all jobs could be replaced by robotic or AI workers. Elon Musk—the real world "Tony Stark" and technology entrepreneur behind Tesla, Hyperloop, and many other disruptive new ventures—believes that robots will outperform humans in every field of activity far faster than we can imagine. Others such as the OECD predict that for every new job created, three or more will disappear through automation.

However, the future is not a statistic. Whilst the cataclysmic "replaced by robots" warnings may well be overstated in the short term, the pace of change will inevitably quicken—a number of job roles are already being transformed by AI technologies in the workplace. Indeed, some jobs could be eliminated entirely while other new work roles will be created. Whether eliminated or transformed, one reasonable take-away remains: AI is recalibrating the division of labor between humans and technology.

To help put the potential changes in an everyday context, here are 20 currently human job roles that could be transformed or eliminated completely by the use AI and robotics over the period from 2020 to 2030:

Public Services

1. Doctors/Surgeons – Fully autonomous and remote controlled robotic surgeons will diagnose, treat and operate on patients in areas where there are no human medics available. Humans might monitor or control these robo-docs via video from central hub hospital facilities in bigger towns and cities. New service propositions might emerge such as autonomous vehicle-based mobile doctors' surgeries which visit the patient to enable remote diagnosis and conversation while the doctor remains in their office.

2. Policing – Robots could perform tasks like crowd control, and police drones could track and intercept criminals escaping from crime scenes. Autonomous police cars could undertake ultra-high-speed chases and then use either robots or drones to detain the occupants without risking human officers' lives.

3. Teachers – A combination of technology advances, changing societal expectations, evolving business needs, and new educational insights mean we can anticipate deep transformations

of the overall educational system and curriculum. As a result, teachers could find their roles being redefined on a regular basis. So, while AI might be in charge of imparting most of the technical skills and information required by learners, educators would focus on developing human-to-human social skills. Life-long learning journeys would also require more insightful and sensitive mentoring capabilities. The teacher could become the nurturer, coach, facilitator, community builder, and therapist.

Professions

4. Journalists – AI tools are already being used to gather, sort, analyze, interpret, and write the resulting articles and reports for online news sites and investment banks. This will extend to drone-based robo-journos sent in to capture and report on the most dangerous situations around the world and to cover a far wider range of situations at far lower cost than dispatching humans to every news scene.

5. Investment Analysts, Fund Managers, and Traders – Invest-ment bots will have the capacity to analyze ever larger volumes of current and historic trading data, news, company updates, and market sector information in a fraction of a second to make investment decisions.

6. Accountants – AI would enable real-time analysis of every transaction as it happens, thus reducing the potential for error and fraud and enabling the maintenance a continuously updated set of transaction accounts without human interven-tion. The ability to track and analyze every commercial and social interaction would create new opportunities for suitably skilled and reputable accountants who can leverage their trustworthiness and experience to become high-level busi-ness and financial advisors. The emphasis would be more on improving business results rather than collating and auditing them. In this role, the keys to a successful career would include understanding the evolving dynamics of a mixed business environment comprising machines and humans, the ability to spot and interpret complex emerging patterns, communication

skills, and creativity.

7. Lawyers – A range of search, analysis, and contract drafting tasks are already being automated. The use of AI across sectors might challenge existing regulations and lead to a whole raft of new legal precedent work requiring expert input. However, the elimination of the potential for human error would decrease the number of legal disputes—as might be expected from the advent of self-driving cars reducing the number of human drivers. Robolawyers are already overturning parking tickets in the UK and US. Additionally, smart policing devices and an expanding blanket of sensors will feed into AI judges where there would be little to no room for debate. Moral and ethical issues related to technology advances may become the next legal growth arena.

8. Life Coaches and Therapists – Automation forecasts today are already causing anxiety and stress among perfectly healthy professionals. When mass layoffs start, society could see mental health issues rise to crisis level. Addressing these issues in a timely manner, promoting coping mechanisms, and highlighting the importance of mental well-being for society would be fundamental priorities for life coaches and therapists. A growing number might choose to become coaches and therapists with the disappearance of their former roles as lawyers, accountants, engineers, doctors, retailers, and taxi drivers.

9. Drivers and Mechanics – From taxis to buses, trucks and rescue services, humans seem likely to be eased out gradually from these roles as regulations allow autonomous/driverless vehicles onto the roads. These new "autonomous people moving units" can be designed around their primary purpose: moving people around on business, on leisure, and on holiday. They hold out the promise of being inherently safer, more fuel efficient, and more productive—freeing up drivers' time. They could also become self-diagnosing and connect with other vehicles to form self-insurance pools. The use of shape shifting 4D-printing techniques could also result in self-repairing vehicles.

Retail, Travel, and Construction

10. Sales Representatives – AI could become the personal shopper of the future, learning our desires and requirements and—over time—making purchases with less and less need to check in with us. Retail algorithms may offer recommendations, drawing on vast databases of consumer preferences and our own shopping history and social media profiles. Shopping could become a task that no longer requires humans to allocate their precious time to do it. For those that still want a say in the process, it would be intertwined with other activities and may only take seconds to complete. For example, films and TV shows would offer the ability to click on an item being worn by an actor to order it. Self-driving devices and drones would then be able to deliver the purchase anytime and anywhere.

11. Concierges – As the traditional concierge figure is increasingly replaced by AI and robots, experiences where every luxurious desire is catered for would become more affordable. AI would take care of everything from suggesting plans and making reservations, to adding room amenities and scheduling rides. New forms of high-end AI could charge a steep premium, and serve as a vehicle for the conspicuous consumption crowd to flaunt their wealth.

12. Travel Agents – From holidays to business travel, AI could increasingly take on the end-to-end booking process. The applications would collate individual, family, and group/event travel preferences, search for options, design highly personalized itineraries, make reservations, and complete the payment on our behalf. Travel agents may need to become application specialists, signposting the best apps for their clients. Other immersive technologies including augmented and virtual reality could provide opportunities for agents to offer a taster experience, allowing travelers to feel the bed linen, smell the bathroom fragrances, and taste the food from a hotel on the other side of the world as part of their client service.

13. Construction Workers – Robotic excavators could undertake trenching work for new construction projects while increasingly sophisticated 3D printing coupled with drones and robotic workers could replace many construction jobs. These might include demolition, bricklaying, plastering, plumbing, cabling, and carpentry. Provision could be made in the 3D-printed construction process for the different properties and materials required—including external weather proofing, preparing internal surfaces for bespoke decoration and finishing which may be completed by robots, and installation of utilities. These construction technologies would be underpinned by AI providing the scope for autonomous construction with minimum human supervision. New materials used in the construction could include self-healing properties and further reduce the reliance on human labor for repair and maintenance throughout the building's life.

Changing Organizational Roles

14. Entrepreneurs and Leaders – Instead of looking for human partners and employees, entrepreneurs might increasingly scout for the combination of AI systems that would match their personality profile and range of business needs better. One-person businesses could be more common as artificial general intelligence materializes—enabling the growth of fully automated decentralized autonomous organizations (DAOs) which have literally no employees.

15. Managers – A vast swathe of management roles could disappear as the workforce they supervise, and most of their own tasks, are automated. Reports, meetings, performance appraisals, and team briefings become a thing of history when you have no staff and no work to do. For those that still have roles, the priority will shift from managing the present to creating the future, designing how work gets done with an in-depth appreciation of the limitations and advantages of AI and human workers alike. However, the pursuit of maximum efficiency would not be enough in a constantly changing world: The requirement to

solve new challenges and realize new potential opportunities will require uniquely human capabilities for some time to come, so truly unleashing human potential would become the new source of competitive advantage.

16. Research and Development – From pharmaceuticals to new materials and electronic devices, AI software is increasingly being used to conduct more and more of the R&D value chain. The use of AI helps compress the iterative innovation process of trial-and-error experimentation. This involves doing more trials faster and comparing real-time data with historic and predictive consumer profiles to better target the solutions. Tailoring products and services using AI might lead organically to the creation of new and better offerings.

17. HR Managers – Employee diversity might take on a new dimension when many business environments include a mix of AI, physical robots, holograms, "standard issue" humans, and those with artificial augmentations of their brains and bodies. Different types of AI would have different jobs to fulfill alongside and—increasingly—in supervision of humans. Recognizing and nurturing the value of humanity in the workplace, helping people retain their worth and dignity, and resolving human-machine disputes could become priority tasks for HR managers to address.

18. Marketing Researchers and Strategists – The data shared by consumers would be automatically analyzed by AI in real time. This feedback loop would create dynamic marketing campaigns able to optimize themselves based on each response. Offers would be tailored to the individual according to both their personal preferences and the time of day when they are most likely to make a purchase.

19. Customer Service Representatives – Chatbots are already making sales calls, helping customers make choices, and solving callers' problems across a wide range of industries. No mood swings, standardized quality, 24/7 availability, and extensive and constant up-to-date knowledge are just a few

of the benefits that AI promises to bring to customer service. However, there might still be delicate and complex issues that would be handled better with a human touch.

20. Personal Assistants – Future generations of Siri, Cortana, and Alexa should be able to undertake personal shopping, screen incoming calls, and determine which news to show us. They could also save our time by sorting and responding to email backlogs and look after our well-being—for example sharing our health and allergy information with a restaurant prior to our visit.

In addition to this top twenty, there are numerous other ways we might anticipate jobs could evolve in the future. Opportunities might arise in areas such as personal trainers, care of the elderly, and the performing arts. We might also see a requirement to help older workers learn about the new and disruptive technologies, and possibly more demand for teachers/classroom facilitators if greater emphasis is placed on developing life skills in smaller-sized, face-to-face classes.

The industries of the future will also generate a significant volume of mainly graduate or master's degree-level opportunities in everything from alternative energy and synthetic materials, to human augmentation and driverless vehicles. As the world becomes increasingly tech-enabled, people might conversely crave live and unaugmented experiences—which could drive a growth in opportunities in bars, restaurants, entertainment experiences, and live performers of all kinds.

Ultimately, today's business leaders acknowledge that the robots are coming; it is just that we don't know where they may have their biggest impacts. Productivity is expected to rise, but what will it mean for actual employee performance, satisfaction, and engagement? How will customer service be different in the AI-powered workforce of the future? What is the role of education and job training in a world with constant fluctuations in business models? To stay ahead of the game, mental exercises like constructing scenarios can provide insights that challenge the expected future and open doors to exciting new images of progress. Visions of the future are empowering tools at a time when drastic changes are afoot, and uncertainty is high. They can help us prepare organizations and individuals for a range of possibilities, and rehearsing the future also helps reduce the shock factor when the more radical developments do play out.

So, will robots take, make, or reboot the future of work? Stay tuned to find out.

- *What are the key factors that should be considered when choosing a future professional career?*
- *For those seeking to make it to the top, what might be the right balance between job-specific technical competencies and more broad-based people skills?*
- *How might we react if AI was able to predict or enforce our ideal career paths, forcing us to fulfill our destiny?*

Hand Picked by Robots – The Beginning of the End for Humans in the Food Sector?

By Rohit Talwar, Steve Wells, and Alexandra Whittington

How might smart technologies impact food and beverage industry jobs in the next 10 years?

The so called Fourth Industrial Revolution is bringing with it successive waves of ever-smarter technologies that could redefine our most basic notions of business, work, employment, wages, government, society, human purpose, and the daily lives of people on this planet. This article explores how such developments could impact the workplace—using the food industry as an example of how deep the applications could go and how wide-ranging the impacts might be.

We're already used to seeing armies of shiny robots undertaking repetitive manufacturing tasks in the food industry—now they are spreading to a variety of roles previously considered the exclusive domain of humans. For example, smart robots and drones are in growing use on farms for a range of tasks from ploughing and planting, to inspection, pruning, and harvesting. El Dulze, a Spanish food processor, now uses robotics to pick up heads of lettuce from a conveyor belt, rejecting those that do not comply with company standards.

In Germany, BratwurstBot takes your order, cooks the sausage to your requirements, and serves it. Artificial intelligence (AI) is used in planning delivery routes and predicting what goods are likely to be in high demand and therefore need to be ordered. In the UK, Honest have launched a totally unmanned, AI-powered coffee kiosk. We are also seeing robots and AI being used in recipe creation, food preparation, bar tending, and table service. New applications in the sector are literally being announced daily.

However, this is just the start; the next waves of development will see the combinatorial effect of AI, robotics, big data, and cloud services working together, creating the opportunity for machines to interact with humans through the provision of services rather than simply delivering us data, analysis, and decision support. Some recent examples of AI in food production include the Hands-Free Hectare project from Harper Adams University, which is farming a plot of land with zero human intervention whatsoever; and Arable, a start-up that hopes to revolutionize the food supply chain with AI-enabled predictive farming.

As the cost of manufacturing robots declines and technological capabilities expand, it's ever more likely that robots will gradually be substituted for labor in a wide range of low-wage service occupations. Imagine a restaurant with humans, augmented humans, robots, holograms, and smart AI table top displays all working in the same space. As a human, do you trust your robot server, chef, and bartender? What happens when the robot is smarter than you, or knows what you want before you do through the use of predictive analytics? Will the AI chef interact directly with the AI-based intelligent agent on your phone to ascertain allergies and intolerances before preparing your meal? Could the bartender and your intelligent agent work together to surprise you with a new cocktail prepared specifically to your taste preferences?

As business leaders and managers, the advent of these new technologies working alongside or in place of humans creates as whole new set of requirements for how we supervise, mentor, motivate, and reward such a blended workforce. The issue of the rights and protections of robots also starts to emerge—many films depict humans trying to sabotage or harm their robot counterparts. Should we try to protect robots and give them similar workplace protections as those who they may be replacing? Furthermore, should we be concerned about the potential risks that could arise from the total automation of our food supply and food chain?

The much cited 2013 study on the *Future of Employment* by Carl Benedikt Frey and Michael Osborne of the Oxford Martin School found that in the food and beverage industry food scientists were the least likely to lose out to computerization whereas fast food workers and coffee shops were among the most likely.[5] It is entirely possible that, in the next 20 years, 80% or more of current jobs in the food and beverage industry could become obsolete, fully or partially automated, or redesigned to eliminate the human component. For those who believe that employment is the preferred future for humanity, the challenge is to ensure that we are doing enough today by encouraging the industries of tomorrow, supporting entrepreneurship and enabling start-ups, preparing the workforce of tomorrow, and re-motivating and reskilling those whose jobs are displaced by automation.

Clearly there will still be a demand for humans in a range of roles that require creativity, innovation, problem-solving, collaboration, and customer engagement. So, we might accept a robo-chef at a fast food outlet where consistency and speed are key; however, when going for more upmarket dining options where talent, inspiration, creativity, and service are the attraction, we think many people would likely prefer a human chef and waiting staff.

Forward-looking industry leaders are already investing the time to understand what's coming over the horizon, experimenting with the technologies, and preparing their staff for change. This includes equipping managers with the skills to help and motivate employees to learn new roles quickly, take up new opportunities, and even start their own business. Helping individuals take control of their own destiny is an increasingly common trait of the enlightened organization.

- *How will the food and beverage industry reinvent itself for the Fourth Revolution?*

- *How might AI change our food routines and indirectly the supply chain and logistics of the industry?*
- *How might AI be used to help address employee learning needs?*

A version of this article was originally published in *Food & Beverage Magazine* under the title "Will we soon see the end of jobs?"

Rethinking Work and Jobs in the Exponential Era

By Steve Wells, Alexandra Whittington, and Rohit Talwar

Will any of the jobs that exist today still be around in 20 years? Is automation destined to rewrite all our futures?

Across society, we are beginning to acknowledge that smart technologies could transform every aspect of business, work, government, and our daily lives. We are already used to seeing faceless robots undertaking repetitive manufacturing tasks, and smart applications determining our credit ratings, autopiloting planes, and delivering an array of functionality to our mobile devices. But this is just the start; the next waves of development will see the coming together of artificial intelligence (AI), robotics, big data, and cloud services. The combinatorial effect of these exponential technologies is really what creates the opportunity for machines to interact with humans through the provision of services rather than simply delivering us data, analysis, and decision support.

If we look further into the future, the workplace of tomorrow is going to be very different from today. Imagine a workplace with humans, augmented humans, robots, holograms, and display-based AI manifestations all working in the same space. As a human, do you trust your robot colleague? What happens when the robot is smarter than you? How will we respond when the AI application working 24/7/365 complains that we are simply not learning or working fast enough to keep up with it? As a Human Resources Manager, how do you manage and monitor such a work force? What happens when the smart robot wants to take a vacation or brings a harassment case against its human colleague?

The Future of Work

It seems that whatever the country, whatever the economic context, the critical question is becoming ever more pertinent: What is the future of work in an era of exponential technology development? Artificial intelligence is arguably the big game changer and becoming more commonplace. We already see narrow AI in use in internet searches, customer targeting applications, and in predictive analytics. But AI has much greater capability that will emerge into every aspect of our lives in the future. Increasingly devices will learn more about us, provide an ever-increasing range of support, and take on more of our tasks. We are automating a lot more activity in literally every sector, and that is set to continue at an accelerating rate.

The goal for some—regarded as unappealing and potentially dangerous by others—is for AI to replicate human intelligence. That does create questions of the balance in society between human and machine. What are the ethical and control questions that need to be answered to ensure we harness the potential of AI in service of society and not just the technology corporations?

Future of Business

At Fast Future, in our recent book *The Future of Business*, we identified thirty different trillion-dollar industry sectors of the future which we grouped into clusters. We expect these clusters and the underlying industries to be impacted radically by exponential technology developments:

- Information and communications;
- Production and construction systems;
- Citizen services and domestic infrastructure;
- New societal infrastructure and services;
- Transformation of existing sectors such accounting, legal, and

financial services; and,

- Energy and environment.

So, we can clearly see the significant disruptive potential that technology offers to emerging sectors and the new players within them. The McKinsey Global Institute made a forecast of which technologies will drive the economy of the future. They predict that mobile internet, the automation of work knowledge, the Internet of things (where many factory, office, and household devices and appliances are connected to the internet), and cloud computing will all form part of a transformative information technology (IT) backdrop and be the most significant creators of new economic value. They also singled out advanced robotics and autonomous vehicles as playing a significant part in future economic growth.

Future Skills and Management Challenges

Given the importance of the issue, it is not surprising that there have been several research projects exploring what this scale of technological change could mean for the future of work.

Pew Research (2014) posed the question, "Will networked, automated, AI and robotic devices have displaced more jobs than they have created by 2025?"[6] Their key findings were:

- 48% of respondents said that robots and digital agents will displace significant numbers of blue-collar and white-collar workers;
- Society would see increases in income inequality, significant numbers of unemployable people, and breakdowns in the social order;
- Conversely, 52% said technology will not displace more jobs than it creates. Lost jobs would be offset by human ingenuity creating new occupations, and industries; and,
- This group also pointed out that current social structures (e.g. education) are not adequately preparing people for the skills needed in the future job market.

A 2013 study on the *Future of Employment* by Carl Benedikt Frey and

Michael Osborne of the Oxford Martin School explored the probability of computerization for 702 occupations and asked, "Which jobs are most vulnerable?"[7] The study found that 47% of workers in the US had jobs at high risk of potential automation. The most at-risk groups were transport and logistics (taxi and delivery drivers), sales and services (cashiers, counter and rental clerks, telemarketers, and accountants), and office support (receptionists and security guards). The equivalent at risk workers were 35% of the workforce in the UK and 49% in Japan.

A 2016 McKinsey Global Institute report looked at the automation of the global economy.[8] The findings were based on a study that explored 54 countries representing 95% of global GDP and more than 2,000 work activities. The study found that the proportion of jobs that can be fully automated by adapting currently demonstrated technology is less than 5%, although for middle-skill categories this could rise to 20%. It also said that based on current technologies, 60% of all jobs have at least 30% of their activities that are technically automatable. The research found that, ultimately, automation technologies could affect 49% of the world economy; 1.1 billion employees and US$12.7 trillion in wages. China, India, Japan, and the US account for more than half of these totals. The report concluded that it would be more than two decades before automation reaches 50% of all of today's work activities.

The World Economic Forum's 2016 study into *The Future of Jobs* saw an increasingly dynamic jobs landscape.[9] It estimated that 65% of children entering primary school today will work in job types that don't yet exist, and that 3.5 times as many jobs could be lost to disruptive labor market changes in the period 2015–2020 than are created. While the study saw job losses in routine white-collar office functions, it saw gains in computing, mathematics, architecture, and engineering related fields.

The report identified several job categories and functions that are expected to become critically important by 2020:

- Data analysts – leveraging big data and AI;
- Specialized sales representatives – commercializing and

articulating new propositions; and,

- Senior managers and leaders – to steer companies through the upcoming change and disruption.

In addition, the report concluded that, "By 2020, more than a third of the desired core skill sets of most occupations will be comprised of skills that are not yet considered crucial to the job today. Social skills—such as persuasion, emotional intelligence, and teaching others—will be in higher demand across industries than narrow technical skills, such as programming or equipment operation and control."

Our own view is that we could well see 80% or more of current jobs disappearing in the next 20 years. Some will become obsolete, others will be fully or partially automated and, in many cases, tasks will be redesigned to eliminate the need for human input and decision making. The big question here is whether these jobs will be replaced by the combination of entrepreneurship, increased investment in education, adult training, human endeavor, and the rise of the six sector clusters described above. While we don't know the answer, we don't have to wait—there is a lot we can do today to prepare for possible disruption.

For example, at the individual level, there are new skills we need to think about acquiring now to equip us for the world of work in the future. We all like to work in a world that is calm, stable, and predictable but the reality is very different. That world is changing ever faster, so we need to become proficient at developing and working with a new set of survival skills for the 21st century which include foresight, curiosity, sense making, accelerated learning, a tolerance of uncertainty, scenario thinking, coping with complexity, and collaborative working.

So What for HR?

We are heading into a world of wicked problems that will require not "Ordinary Management," but "Extraordinary Leadership." The leadership and management style required when working in uncertain situations can be challenging. For Ordinary Management we apply accepted best practice approaches; it's the domain of trend extrapolation, tame problems, and technical challenges. But in the increasingly disruption filled world we are heading into, we require Extraordinary Leadership because our challenges are difficult or impossible to solve due to unpredictable trend paths, incomplete and contradictory information, and changing requirements that are often difficult to define or agree upon. We need the ability to navigate a rapidly changing reality, make decisions with imperfect information, and to tune our intuition to "sense and respond" when surrounded by an array of relatively weak signals of what might happen next.

A critical requirement here is to determine the organizational capacity to work in new ways including envisioning the future and making sense of complexity—it seems to us that HR could play a big role in developing these core capabilities.

We are in a rapidly changing world, one that is increasingly technology driven, one that will host more generations in parallel—with their divergent work/life wants and needs—than we have seen before. One that is highly likely to see a revolutionary change in jobs as we know them today, one that will see the birth of new jobs, and the demise of others. One that could ultimately see not working as the new normal.

- *How is HR helping to create a generationally and technologically diverse culture?*

- *What role is HR playing in driving culture changes that help align the organization with the constantly evolving interplay between customer strategies, their resulting requirements, and our own business propositions and capabilities?*

- *How is HR using technology to streamline and automate activities such as performance management, learning and development, resource planning, and sourcing and thus free up time for these more strategic tasks by?*

- *Is there an opportunity for the Human Resources function to transition to one of Resource Management—adopting a more business-wide strategic role—to meet the organization's business objectives?*

Hire the Robots, Free the People

By Rohit Talwar, Steve Wells, and Alexandra Whittington

How might AI and the end of jobs liberate future generations?

With the rise of artificial intelligence (AI) and other smart technologies, it is inevitable that many jobs will be automated away. At one level, such technological unemployment is nothing new. From the advent of the steam engine and mechanization of farming, through to the robotization of car manufacturing and introduction of personal computing, jobs have always been automated by technology. Historically, this hasn't been an issue—as new technologies have come to market, human ingenuity and the ability to create new products and services have, until now, increased the scope for employment and fulfillment.

However, things could be markedly different this time round—regular forecasts suggest the vast majority of all current jobs could be impacted or disappear through automation. Furthermore, perhaps only a fraction of those displaced will find opportunities in the highly automated growth industries of the future. This need not be a problem if we can wean ourselves off the notion of having a job as being the ultimate goal and responsibility of every individual of working age. Such a mindset and cultural transition is not without challenges. Current and critical social structures such as education, training, the welfare state, and the benefits system are clearly not fit for purpose in a jobless future. However, for future generations, this may be a blessing in disguise.

The End of Jobs?

Much of the current debate on automation focuses on the demise of existing jobs across great swathes of economic activity. The traditional loss of jobs to automation in manufacturing looks set to accelerate, and the incursion of automation into the service and white-collar sectors is gathering momentum. Can automation really replace—as some have predicted—up to 80% or more of existing jobs?

What if we were to experience this most extreme outcome from robotics and automation in the workplace and reach a point where the majority of people become technologically unemployed? How quickly would governments respond? How quickly might society redefine the notion of unemployment to have less negative connotations? What would people do all day? How would they make a living, or would this phrase become meaningless? Assuming technological unemployment impacts 80-90% of jobs—the most severe forecast—how would the majority of people survive without some form of income? And what would we do with our time (and the rest of our lives) if not employed? These questions require a societal response.

A Global "Mincome"

In twenty years, automation may have created a society where jobs aren't available or are not being created at the scale necessary to employ the large numbers of people digitized out of a job. Employment would become a rare and specialized activity, creating huge groups of people with no job, no prospects, and no income. Governments would be forced to implement programs to relieve the economic and societal pressures that could arise: How would people buy food, pay rent, obtain education? Even more so, how would they buy the products and services—produced by the robots—that companies sell?

One of the more humane solutions proposes aggressive public policy to underpin a post-job society with basic income programs, known as universal basic income (UBI) or "mincome" ("minimum income") and universal basic services (transport, electricity, education, sanitation, healthcare). If AI and other forms of smart technology do take over many work functions, the social safety net would need to expand beyond filling temporary gaps to forming the basis of the provision of essential needs for most people.

Today's social safety nets are designed to protect the lowest-earning and non-earning members of the community, mostly on a temporary basis: The nature of unemployment benefits, rehabilitation, and job training programs paid for with public funds is that they are intended to encourage people back to work. Establishing a mincome for all could empower the majority and protect society from collapse due to economic imbalance. In fact, rather than provide bare subsistence, in a society where technology has enabled abundance, a mincome might offer the support needed to foster human creativity, problem solving, and innovation. Making sure all the basic needs are met across society would be a necessity in the absence of paying jobs. This could also provide a huge benefit to society in terms of maximizing human potential.

Education for the Post-Jobs World

Though many future of work predictions are foreboding, they are not death sentences. As far as the automation of mainstream work goes, we already see losses in routine white-collar office functions, but gains in computing, mathematical, architecture, and engineering related roles. However, in a future environment where machines are doing more of the process element of most roles, then social skills—such as persuasion, caregiving, emotional intelligence, and teaching—could well be in higher demand than narrow technical skills.

Recent evidence bears out the claim that teachers will be in high demand. Indeed, UNESCO has estimated that almost 70 million teachers must be recruited to achieve the goal of universal primary and secondary education by 2030. While AI might perform the logistical and technical aspects of teaching, and especially grading and assessing, there is no adequate concept yet for automating one-on-one human support in the classroom. Rather than panic at the thought of law firms replacing attorneys with robolawyers, we might see instead an opportunity to increase the number of smart people working with children. Automation could make teaching a more attractive and lucrative profession, and drive innovation in schools by enhancing human skills in the classroom.

More generally, are education systems ready to respond to the shifting nature of work and the disappearance of jobs? What is the justification for compulsory schooling, for example, in a future where jobs don't exist? Contextual awareness and broader social competence may become the priority for schooling institutions when the technology can deliver the technical content. Schools will have to change to adapt to new realities, which could include lawyers teaching civics, social workers taking kids on field trips into at-risk communities, and scientists escorting children to conduct experiments on local waste sites.

Though AI will absorb the brunt of the informational and computational work, human insight will be vital when it comes to complex human and social problems, including the environment. AI will take jobs, but can also help ensure that education systems promote human creativity and provide insights and awareness that can be used for developing solutions that overcome some of the world's most demanding problems.

Robots Taking Jobs – The Ultimate Win-Win?

The challenges we describe are not new. Indeed, for several generations now, outdated formal schooling has occupied the most developmental years of a person's life under the premise of being preparation for future employment. Yet, technology trends suggest that the jobs we prepare our children for today won't be there in ten or twenty years. As outlined, employment automation trends seem to point to the need for highly human capacities in the coming decades, suggesting that communications, caring, facilitating, conflict resolution, and problem-solving are core skills around which to design modern education systems.

Without clear-cut jobs to prepare for, future generations, enabled with some form of mincome, would then be in a position where experiential and self-guided learning could be more embedded in everyday life and become the new definition of "making a living." Rather than spend eight hours a day in classrooms, in preparation for spending eight hours a day on a job, children could go outdoors, explore their communities, and travel short and long distances to learn about things they enjoy. Future generations could experience education that preserves humanity, not eliminates it.

There is unlimited potential for humanity in a world where work is mostly performed by machines and algorithms. One of the most positive responses to automation would be to eliminate the vast disparities in social and economic equality. In particular, our biggest gifts to future generations would be to redirect resources to ensure all people have what they need to survive, and provide opportunities so that the majority, not the lucky few, get to seek personal fulfillment. We have a choice in front of us today: use the technology at hand to create massive unemployment and economic inequality, or as an enabler of abundance and human potential.

The very same exponential technologies that could replace humans will also enable the creation of new businesses. They provide scope for creating innovative business models to bring products and services to market for a customer base who will be working in jobs that do not exist yet. Preparing future generations for tomorrow's jobs, or the absence of work altogether, is one of the main challenges of the future. It is also one of the biggest opportunities.

- *How might we rethink society based around our emerging concepts of the future of work, inequality, and the role of education?*
- *What would it take to harness AI to bring real freedom to humanity?*
- *How might different societies with different histories, social values, and cultures react to and prepare for future waves of changes in a globalized world?*

Taxing the Robots – Far Sighted or Fanciful?

By Rohit Talwar, Steve Wells, and Alexandra Whittington

Are robot taxes a plausible solution for the upcoming wave of technological unemployment?

When you know a storm is coming, you have a sense of its likely form, speed, direction, potential impact, and possible duration. Armed with that knowledge you can then take in provisions, batten down the hatches, and go to a place of safety. The challenge takes on a wholly different magnitude when that storm is in the form of artificial intelligence (AI) software that might power smart or even superintelligent machines and robots which could in turn impact every aspect of life on the planet. So, what's really going on here and why are we talking about robot taxes as a solution to the potential rise in long-term unemployment? Here we explore ten key questions to help the reader get their head around the whole subject of taxing the "bots."

1. What's driving the debate?

The big issue here is the likely extent to which automation will reshape the industrial landscape, change the nature of work as we know it, and drive up the number of people facing permanent unemployment. On the one hand, we know smart technologies are developing at an exponential rate. Individually and when combined, they will have an impact from automated warehouses and autonomous cars, to computerized drug discovery and the diagnosis of Alzheimer's disease ten years before the symptoms show—it's already happening. However, and crucially, we don't know how far and how fast AI and these other disruptive technologies will spread. Furthermore, we don't know how many jobs they will take out; we don't know how society will respond (e.g. the Uber backlash); we don't know the extent to which firms will retain people when they automate; we don't know how fast the new sectors will grow; and we don't know how many new jobs they will create. In practice we are pretty clueless—but that's understandable at this stage in the development of such a powerful technology.

2. So why act now?

What we do know is that jobs are already going, more will follow, and it would be a reckless government and a careless citizenry that didn't think about how to address the challenges. Countries already know that to compete in the emerging global economy, we need to change the nature and focus of education at all levels and prepare adults for roles in the new sectors—which will mainly be higher skilled as the "bots" will most likely do the rest. So, it's reasonable to at least explore the scenario of rising technological unemployment over the next decade. Realistically, in the United Kingdom (UK) for example, this means we'd need to fund either a higher total unemployment benefit bill or the provision of some form of guaranteed basic income and/or guaranteed basic services. In this scenario, fewer people working means they are likely to be paying less overall income tax, which means we must fund the revenue shortfall somehow—that's assuming we want to maintain the current level of public service provision whilst also covering the higher unemployment costs.

3. How are governments responding?

Let's look at the UK as an example of how governments are wrestling with the issue—the range of responses is not untypical of how different nations are approaching it. The ruling Conservative Party is loath to acknowledge the possibility of rising unemployment due to automation. The hope is that encouragement of free markets and lower corporate tax rates will drive business growth and employment. They believe that unemployment costs will be met through revenues from corporate and individual taxes coupled with Valued Added Tax (VAT).

In contrast, rising numbers of young members in the opposition Labour Party are concerned about the impact on their future—spurred on by already high levels of youth and graduate unemployment. They are keen to ensure the UK doesn't go into the kind of decline in youth opportunity that we saw with Greece and Spain.

In response, and acknowledging the fundamental changes taking place in the industrial economy, Labour has been mooting the idea of "robot taxes" to finance the cost of adult retraining, education transformation, investment in new technology sectors, and unemployment provisions. The argument is that robots should be taxed because they will be considered as something that creates value for the owner, like property, and if firms are cutting headcounts, then they are likely to be making higher profits. Furthermore, the belief is that those who will receive the benefits will spend that money with the firms who paid the robot taxes.

4. What would robot taxes pay for?

Clearly, the primary purpose should be to address the societal consequences of job automation. So, the most obvious application would be to fund unemployment benefits or guaranteed incomes and services. However, it is difficult to believe that any tax raised could be permanently and transparently allocated by government for one specific use or another. In the UK for example, when one looks across the range of taxes now, is there evidence to show that fuel duty is ploughed back into highway maintenance as originally envisaged?

Alongside unemployment costs, there is a strong argument that a significant proportion of the revenue from robot taxes should be channeled directly into public education. This would create a positive role for robots in society, which would be to pay for public schools and universities. The hope is that this would prevent a backlash from the people whose jobs are lost to automation. Ideally, it would also generate enough money to revamp an outdated education system into a forward looking one that teaches the knowledge and skills which will be in demand in 2030 and beyond, when most jobs as we now know them may have been absorbed by robots and algorithms.

A robot tax could help pay for a new approach to education which develops the whole person, not just the future worker. These would include life skills (e.g. cooking, health, and household management), interpersonal skills (listening, leadership, and writing), and self-awareness (mindfulness meditation and mental health strategies). The underlying principle is that we should use the value of automation to benefit society and prevent future problems.

5. What is the likelihood of governments around the world introducing a robot tax on companies that replace humans with smart machines?

The South Korean government has reduced tax allowances for those investing in job-replacing automation, which effectively amounts to a new robot tax for those previously claiming the allowance. Several governments have started to think about the spending side of the equation—the human consequences of automation—exploring everything from new approaches to adult education to encouraging the creation of start-ups. Several, such as Canada, Finland, and Germany, have also been experimenting with different forms of guaranteed or universal basic income (UBI).

These are relatively small experiments; the intention is to learn about them before they are required. The experiments are looking at different funding models, whether any access conditions should be applied, and the impact on mental health, domestic violence, crime, and community cohesion. Such experimentation seems eminently sensible as an input to any nation's debate on the topic.

At a broader tax policy level, across the world, rapid automation must be seen as one very important driver of change to nations' tax collection regimes. Clearly the public spending policy decisions of these governments will also have an impact. Hence it becomes critical to explore different possible scenarios to understand the likely spending requirements and revenues under a range of different conditions. Governments can then examine both their spending priorities and possible revenue instruments. As such, it may be that the impact of automation plays a much bigger role in driving future decisions around taxation policy, broadening the debate beyond the deployment and taxation of robots.

6. Who might lead the way and when might it happen?

It seems unlikely that any government would introduce these kinds of measures within the next two to five years, but by 2030 the possible pace of change means they could well be commonplace in many industrial nations. Countries that are embracing automation and the digital era in all its forms such as South Korea, Japan, and Singapore might be among the first to implement some form of explicit automation taxation mechanism. Whilst China is saying little right now, it has the capacity to enact policy rapidly should the need arise.

The overt and hidden political power of the Indian super-corporates means it is likely to be a very late adopter. In Europe, nations such as Estonia, Finland, Sweden, Denmark, Iceland, and Germany are likely to be among the first to revamp their tax systems in this way. Whilst many in Silicon Valley argue in favor of robot taxes, the US is likely to face strong resistance to such changes. Indeed, it could well be among the last to go down this route and might conceivably not do so at all without a fundamental change in its governance and electoral systems.

7. How might such taxes work in practice?

The going in point here should be to evolve a more flexible approach to creating government income to fund future public services. The basis of corporate taxation could become even more complex with systems applying AI to large multi-variable data sets to establish a tax liability based on the sector, revenues/profits per employee, the number of people employed, and geographic location. The algorithms could also take account of factors such as expenditure on training and retraining current and former employees, the support given by firms to start-ups, the level of employment created further down the value chain, and the amount of tax paid by the firm's employees.

Perhaps evaluation of a business's broader impact on society could also be factored into determining the level of taxation applied to its profits. Such factors might include the actual level of human employment, local and national social responsibility, and environmental impact—so that the tax paid is based on the net outcomes for a country of a business's operation across a range of different domains.

Some measure of net added value could also be considered. For example, a firm may train its employees so well that they go on to higher paying jobs elsewhere or to generate employment and tax revenues by starting their own business. How might their taxation be assessed relative to a firm who invests little in people development and whose staff cannot find jobs elsewhere when made redundant? In the UK, the Pay as You Earn (PAYE) system is a government mechanism by which employers collect tax from employees and transfer it to the tax authorities. This could be used to calculate credits for application against a business's corporation tax liability.

An interesting scenario to explore would be the possibility that AI could create the opportunity for governments to recover public spending commitments pro-rata from every tax payer and corporation in the country, purely based on individual incomes or business revenues. In the worst-case scenario, this could mean firms posting a loss because they failed to make a profit after paying their fair share for running the country. The key here is modeling a variety of different approaches to see which produces the fairest and most transparent system. This may well evolve over time as the controlling AI algorithm learns about what second and third order behaviors it engenders in firms as they try and reduce their tax bill.

There are, however, precedents we can learn from. For example, the UK pharmaceutical industry has paid a levy based on revenue or capital employed on its supplies to the National Health Service (NHS) with a series of allowable and dis-allowable expenses. This approach has been designed as a mechanism to control profits on medicine supplies to the NHS while seeking to reward investment in R&D. A similar approach could be taken with companies and the level of automation they employ versus their investment in people.

8. What potential risks and drawbacks are there?

Whilst there will be supporters of the idea, this is going to be hugely controversial and unpopular with a lot of politicians, businesses, commentators, accountancy firms, certain news media, and many economists. It is already being cast as unbridled socialism, communism, or Marxism by many proponents of low taxes and free markets. However, at present, no viable alternatives are being put on the table.

At the operational level, it could be costly and complex to implement, and opponents will look for any shortcomings to cast it off as a failure. The prevailing corporate mind-set is often to base multinational operations in lower tax markets, so competition for the hosting of multinational organizations could intensify without global agreements. Inevitably, many will look for ways to minimize their tax payments and a range of advisory services and schemes will spring up to help firms do so. Failure to implement a viable system or a workable alternative could have disastrous consequences for governments, leading to potential reductions in public service provision and even the failure of some economies.

9. What are the potential benefits?

A solution will be required if unemployment does rise and government revenues decline because of lower personal tax and VAT/sales tax income. Whilst robot taxes may not be the ultimate answer, and better solutions might emerge, it is the only clear policy idea that is even being mooted today for what is an increasingly pressing societal issue. Ultimately, the notion of taxation based on automation could prove to be a catalyst for more socially responsible "carrot and stick" approaches to corporate tax.

Maybe the application of increasingly sophisticated AI could be the critical enabling technology to providing a fair and transparent system with no potential for tax avoidance or manipulation by individual firms. Indeed, AI could one day give us even smarter tax systems that none of us can even imagine today. Perhaps the fully automated corporation or decentralized autonomous organization (DAO) of the future may see its prime directive to serve humanity as a whole and maximize its contribution to society.

10. How do we get started?

We don't know yet what robot taxes might look like in practice because no one has really tried to create one. Thus, the first stage must be to run some serious computer simulations of different scenarios for the potential pace of automation and the impacts on employment in different countries around the world. These could be used as input to the development of economic models to explore the funding requirements of different public service strategies and how they might be met. If there's a shortfall between what's required and what could be collected under the current taxation regime, then the potential for different robot tax models (and any alternatives) could be evaluated and the likely implications assessed.

Artificial intelligence is creating the tools that are driving the pace of automation and the prospect of increased unemployment. Equally, AI tools could also be used to design and develop new approaches to taxation that could help us address the societal consequences of technological disruption and ensure a very human future for all.

- *What are the critical questions and concerns we need to explore in the design of robot tax experiments?*
- *If companies could allocate the money collected from robot taxes, what might be the most popular options for how it is spent and why?*
- *What alternative mechanisms to robot taxes might we adopt to provide and fund public services and social protection?*

References

[1 2 8]A future that works: Automation, employment and productivity. McKinsey. https://www.mckinsey.com/~/media/McKinsey/Global%20Themes/Digital%20Disruption/Harnessing%20automation%20for%20a%20future%20that%20works/MGI-A-future-that-works_In-brief.ashx

[3]Technology, jobs and the future of work. McKinsey. 2016 https://www.mckinsey.com/~/media/mckinsey/global%20themes/employment%20and%20growth/technology%20jobs%20and%20the%20future%20of%20work/mgi-technology-jobs-and-the-future-of-work.ashx

[4 5 7]The Future of Employment: How susceptible are jobs to computerization? Carl Benedikt Frey and Michael Osborne. 2013 https://www.oxfordmartin.ox.ac.uk/downloads/academic/The_Future_of_Employment.pdf

[6]AI, Robotics, and the Future of Jobs. Pew Research Center. 2014. http://www.pewinternet.org/2014/08/06/future-of-jobs/

[9]The Future of Jobs. World Economic Forum. 2016. http://www3.weforum.org/docs/WEF_Future_of_Jobs.pdf

Fast Future

Fast Future is a professional foresight firm specializing in delivering keynote speeches, executive education, research, and consulting on the emerging future and the impacts of change for global clients. In 2015 we created a new model of publishing led by three futurists—Rohit Talwar, Steve Wells, and April Koury. As a publisher, our goal is to profile the latest thinking of established and emerging futurists, foresight researchers, and future thinkers from around the world, and to make those ideas accessible to the widest possible audience in the shortest possible time.

Our *FutureScapes* book series is designed to address a range of critical agenda setting futures topics with in-depth contributions from global thought leaders and cutting-edge future thinkers. We cover topics that we believe are relevant to individuals, governments, businesses, and civil society. Our *Fast Future* series is designed to provide rapid insights into the emerging future with a collection of short, hard hitting articles that explore different trends, developments, forces, and ideas shaping the future and how we can respond in a manner that best serves humanity.

Our first book, *The Future of Business*, provides 60 fast moving chapters and 566 pages of cutting-edge thinking from 62 future thinkers in 21 different countries on four continents. Traditional publishers would take two years to deliver a book of this magnitude; we completed the journey from idea to publication in just 19 weeks.

We have also created an innovative business model that bypasses most of the traditional publishing practices and inefficiencies, embracing digital era exponential thinking and applying it to transform the publishing process, the distribution approach, and the profit sharing model. Our publishing model ensures that our authors, core team members, and partners on each book share in its success. Additionally, a proportion of profits are allocated to a development fund to finance causes related to the core topic.

We hope that our story and our approach to publishing are an inspiring example of how business is evolving and being reinvented in the digital era.

Over the coming years, Fast Future aims to publish the work of insightful and inspiring futurists and future thinkers. We are keen to receive proposals from potential authors and those interested in compiling and editing multi-contributor book as part of the *FutureScapes* and *Fast Future* series.

For corporate or bulk orders of *Beyond Genuine Stupidity, The Future of Business,* and *Technology vs. Humanity,* please contact karolina@fastfuture.com.

To book a keynote speaker, discuss an executive education, consulting, or research requirement, or explore partnership opportunities please contact rohit@fastfuture.com.

To submit a chapter idea or a book proposal, discuss ideas for curating and editing a multi-contributor project, or to enquire about permanent and internship opportunities, please contact info@fastfuture.com.

You can learn more about us at www.fastfuture.com.

We look forward to hearing from you!

Also from Fast Future

THE FUTURE OF BUSINESS - Critical insights to a rapidly changing world from 62 future thinkers

The Future of Business is aimed at the leaders of today and the pioneers of tomorrow. Our intention is to provide a broad perspective on the key forces, trends, developments, and ideas that could redefine our world over the next two decades. The goal is to highlight how these future factors are shaping the opportunities, challenges, implications, and resulting choices for those driving the future of business. The book draws on the ideas of 62 futurists, future thinkers and experts in a range of domains from 22 countries on four continents.

The Future of Business highlights how—in a world of constant and ever-more fundamental change—those charged with leadership, management and stewardship of large and small organizations alike are faced with a set of questions many of us never thought we would have to confront. These questions are becoming more prominent and real as we develop a better understanding of, and feeling for, the disruptive potential of what's coming over the horizon.

The Future of Business explores the innovations driving our changing context. Throughout history, people have understood that tomorrow's business landscape will be shaped and influenced by the world around us. What is perhaps different today is the sheer speed at which our world is being transformed by a convergence of science-led innovations and the ideas they enable. We are entering a fascinating period in our history, where science and the technologies it spawns, are now at the heart of the agenda.

The Future of Business is designed to provide wide ranging visions of future possibilities and take us on a tour of the forces shaping the political, economic, and social environment. We explore the advances in science and technology that could have the greatest impact on society and drive business disruption. We examine the implications of these for how business will need to evolve and the new industries that could emerge over the next two decades. We highlight key tools, approaches, and ways of thinking about the future that can help organizations embed foresight at the heart of the management model. We conclude with a framework that highlights key choices we face in shaping *The Future of Business*.

Visit www.fastfuture.com for more information.

THE FUTURE REINVENTED – Reimagining Life, Society, and Business

The second book in the *Fast Future* series explores the future transformations that could arise from the disruptive technological, scientific, social, and economic developments shaping the decade ahead. The authors offer a range of unique visions of different aspects of a future in which the very tenets of reality are undergoing deep and vital transformations. Through a series of chapters organized into three sections (transformations in life, industries, and business), they present holistic future scenarios that encourage strategic thinking about what lies beyond the hype.

Using a long-term futurist perspective, *The Future Reinvented* offers glimpses of the future in different business sectors such as legal, automotive, and sales as well as in different areas of everyday life like retirement, education, and health. Audiences will appreciate the vivid imagery which brings to life a number of different "futures," including workplace scenarios where people work side by side with artificial intelligence or robotic colleagues, can obtain physical enhancements to become smarter, stronger, or more psychologically resilient, or reside in a post-jobs world. The book provides a solid foundation for scenario thinking and planning, identifying signals of change, and interpreting signposts that serve as early warning signs for emerging futures.

The *Fast Future* Book Series

This series of books is designed to provide clear and rapid insights into the trends, forces, developments, and ideas shaping the future and the possible scenarios that could arise. Each book contains a collection of short, hard hitting articles that explore different aspects of the emerging future and how we can respond in a manner that best serves humanity. The books are deliberately intended to be a rapid read—providing the reader with key information needed to get up to speed on relevant future issues—explaining what they are, and their possible implications for individuals, society, business, and government. The first two titles in the series are *Beyond Genuine Stupidity - Ensuring AI Serves Humanity* and *The Future Reinvented - Reimagining Life, Society, and Business.*

Visit www.fastfuture.com for more information.

Available in 2018 from Fast Future

UNLEASHING HUMAN POTENTIAL – The Future of AI in Business

The pace of business investment in and adoption of artificial intelligence (AI) is accelerating and the level of interest and activity is rising across all sectors.

The intention is to provide a diverse set of perspectives on where the technology is going, how it is being deployed in business today, and how the capabilities, applications, and impact of AI could evolve over the next 3-10 years.

The book is designed to have the broadest possible scope and will be co-edited by Rohit Talwar and April Koury.

The book addresses the following key topics:

- The role of AI as a catalyst of the fourth industrial revolution; providing a paradigm shift comparable to mass production or the Internet, not a phase akin to "the cloud"
- How AI capabilities, tools, and technologies could evolve over the next 3-10 years
- Being human and the boundary between humans and machines
- Future potential applications across a range of business sectors for the various branches of AI—including machine learning, deep learning, natural language processing, cognitive computing, robotics and processing of voice, speech, images and video
- The potential impacts, business benefits, and challenges that could arise
- The importance of an organization's internal culture to the speed and breadth of AI implementation
- The power of AI to help unlock the true potential of people in the workplace

- The potential of AI to transform, reshape, and even create entire industries and economies
- Possible impacts of AI on employment and how society might respond
- Potential legal, moral, and ethical issues that could arise from the acceleration of adoption of AI
- Alternative perspectives on the perception of AI in some sections of the media as a force for evil and destroyer of jobs.

Visit www.fastfuture.com for more information.

50:50 – Scenarios for the Next 50 Years

This book explores scenarios for the next 50 years, with 50 perspectives on possible futures from 50 different future thinkers around the world.

The book is designed to have the broadest possible scope and is edited by global futurists Rohit Talwar, Steve Wells, April Koury, and Alexandra Whittington. The book explores potential future scenarios over the next 50 years across a range of topic areas including:

- Macro perspectives on the future
- People and demographics
- Being human and the boundary between humans and machines
- Values, ethics and beliefs
- Civil society: education, healthcare, communities
- Leisure, entertainment, media, and sport
- Government, economics, and legal systems
- Peace, justice, security, and conflict
- Travel and transport
- Energy and environment
- Industries of the future
- Business, work, and jobs
- Science and technology: current, emerging, and yet to be created

A VERY HUMAN FUTURE – Pathways to Sustainable Abundance

A Very Human Future will explore how we can put humanity at the center of the story and harness advances in science and technology in service of the greater social good.

Under Consideration

The landscape for potential publication topics is evolving rapidly and we are excited at the prospects of working on multi-author books under the *FutureScapes* and *Fast Future* series banners or partnering with innovative organizations who share our passion for exploring the future. We are currently considering books on a range of future related themes.

We are always interested to hear from authors who want to bring their ideas, knowledge, and insights to market with Fast Future.

Visit www.fastfuture.com for more information.